A Midsummer Night's Dream

The Taming of the Shrew

As You Like It

William Shakespeare

Illustrations by John Gilbert

D0124948

Copyright © 2007 J. W. Edwards, Inc.
Case design by Denise Kennedy © 2007 J. W. Edwards, Inc.

All rights reserved under International and Pan American
Copyright Conventions.

No part of this book may be reproduced or transmitted
in any form or by any means electronic or mechanical
including photocopying, recording, or by any
information storage and retrieval system,
without permission in writing
from the publisher.

Please direct sales or editorial inquiries to:
BordersTradeBookInventoryQuestions@bordersgroupinc.com

This edition is published by
Borders Classics, an imprint of Borders Group, Inc.,
by special arrangement with
Ann Arbor Media Group, LLC
2500 South State Street, Ann Arbor, MI 48104

Printed and bound in the United States of America
by Edwards Brothers, Inc.

ISBN 13: 978-1-58726-514-3

10   09   08   07   10 9 8 7 6 5 4 3 2 1

Contents

A Midsummer Night's Dream

A Midsummer Night's Dream

Dramatis Personae

Theseus, Duke of Athens
Hippolyta, Queen of the Amazons, betrothed to
    Theseus
Philostrate, Master of the Revels
Egeus, father of Hermia
Hermia, daughter of Egeus, in love with Lysander
Lysander, in love with Hermia
Demetrius, in love with Hermia and favored by Egeus
Helena, in love with Demetrius
Oberon, King of the Fairies
Titania, Queen of the Fairies
Puck, or *Robin Goodfellow*
Peaseblossom, Cobweb, Mote, Mustardseed, fairies at-
    tending Titania
Other *fairies* attending
Peter Quince, a carpenter, representing *Prologue*
Nick Bottom, a weaver, representing *Pyramus*
Francis Flute, a bellows mender, representing *Thisbe*
Tom Snout, a tinker, representing *Wall*
Snug, a joiner, representing *Lion*
Robin Starveling, a tailor, representing *Moonshine*
Lords and Attendants on Theseus and Hippolyta

Scene: Athens, and a wood near it

1.1 ENTER THESEUS, HIPPOLYTA, [AND PHILOSTRATE,]
WITH OTHERS.

Theseus
>Now, fair Hippolyta, our nuptial hour
>Draws on apace. Four happy days bring in
>Another moon; but, O, methinks, how slow
>This old moon wanes! She lingers my desires,
>Like to a stepdame or a dowager
>Long withering out a young man's revenue.

Hippolyta
>Four days will quickly steep themselves in night;
>Four nights will quickly dream away the time;
>And then the moon, like to a silver bow
>New bent in heaven, shall behold the night
>Of our solemnities.

Theseus   Go, Philostrate,
>Stir up the Athenian youth to merriments.
>Awake the pert and nimble spirit of mirth.
>Turn melancholy forth to funerals;
>The pale companion is not for our pomp.

>   [*Exit Philostrate.*]

>Hippolyta, I wooed thee with my sword
>And won thy love doing thee injuries;
>But I will wed thee in another key,
>With pomp, with triumph, and with reveling.

>   *Enter Egeus and his daughter Hermia,*
>   *and Lysander, and Demetrius.*

Egeus
>Happy be Theseus, our renownèd duke!

Theseus
>Thanks, good Egeus. What's the news with thee?

Egeus
>Full of vexation come I, with complaint
>Against my child, my daughter Hermia.—

Stand forth, Demetrius.—My noble lord,
This man hath my consent to marry her.—
Stand forth, Lysander.—And, my gracious Duke,
This man hath bewitched the bosom of my child.
Thou, thou Lysander, thou hast given her rhymes
And interchanged love tokens with my child.
Thou hast by moonlight at her window sung
With feigning voice verses of feigning love,
And stol'n the impression of her fantasy
With bracelets of thy hair, rings, gauds, conceits,
Knacks, trifles, nosegays, sweetmeats—messengers
Of strong prevailment in unhardened youth.
With cunning hast thou filched my daughter's heart,
Turned her obedience, which is due to me,
To stubborn harshness. And, my gracious Duke,
Be it so she will not here before Your Grace
Consent to marry with Demetrius,
I beg the ancient privilege of Athens:
As she is mine, I may dispose of her,
Which shall be either to this gentleman
Or to her death, according to our law
Immediately provided in that case.

Theseus

What say you, Hermia? Be advised, fair maid.
To you your father should be as a god—
One that composed your beauties, yea, and one
To whom you are but as a form in wax
By him imprinted, and within his power
To leave the figure or disfigure it.
Demetrius is a worthy gentleman.

Hermia

So is Lysander.

Theseus   In himself he is;
But in this kind, wanting your father's voice,
The other must be held the worthier.

Hermia

    I would my father looked but with my eyes.

Theseus

    Rather your eyes must with his judgment look.

Hermia

    I do entreat Your Grace to pardon me.

    I know not by what power I am made bold,

    Nor how it may concern my modesty

    In such a presence here to plead my thoughts;

    But I beseech Your Grace that I may know

    The worst that may befall me in this case

    If I refuse to wed Demetrius.

Theseus

    Either to die the death or to abjure

    Forever the society of men.

    Therefore, fair Hermia, question your desires,

    Know of your youth, examine well your blood,

    Whether, if you yield not to your father's choice,

    You can endure the livery of a nun,

    For aye to be in shady cloister mewed,

    To live a barren sister all your life,

    Chanting faint hymns to the cold fruitless moon.

    Thrice blessèd they that master so their blood

    To undergo such maiden pilgrimage;

    But earthlier happy is the rose distilled

    Than that which, withering on the virgin thorn,

    Grows, lives, and dies in single blessedness.

Hermia

    So will I grow, so live, so die, my lord,

    Ere I will yield my virgin patent up

    Unto his lordship, whose unwishèd yoke

    My soul consents not to give sovereignty.

Theseus

    Take time to pause, and by the next new moon—

    The sealing day betwixt my love and me

    For everlasting bond of fellowship—

Upon that day either prepare to die
For disobedience to your father's will,
Or else to wed Demetrius, as he would,
Or on Diana's altar to protest
For aye austerity and single life.

Demetrius
    Relent, sweet Hermia, and, Lysander, yield
    Thy crazèd title to my certain right.

Lysander
    You have her father's love, Demetrius;

Let me have Hermia's. Do you marry him.

Egeus

Scornful Lysander! True, he hath my love,
And what is mine my love shall render him.
And she is mine, and all my right of her
I do estate unto Demetrius.

Lysander

I am, my lord, as well derived as he,
As well possessed; my love is more than his;
My fortunes every way as fairly ranked,
If not with vantage, as Demetrius';
And, which is more than all these boasts can be,
I am beloved of beauteous Hermia.
Why should not I then prosecute my right?
Demetrius, I'll avouch it to his head,
Made love to Nedar's daughter, Helena,
And won her soul; and she, sweet lady, dotes,
Devoutly dotes, dotes in idolatry
Upon this spotted and inconstant man.

Theseus

I must confess that I have heard so much,
And with Demetrius thought to have spoke thereof;
But, being overfull of self-affairs,
My mind did lose it. But, Demetrius, come,
And come, Egeus, you shall go with me;
I have some private schooling for you both.
For you, fair Hermia, look you arm yourself
To fit your fancies to your father's will,
Or else the law of Athens yields you up—
Which by no means we may extenuate—
To death or to a vow of single life.
Come, my Hippolyta. What cheer, my love?
Demetrius and Egeus, go along.
I must employ you in some business
Against our nuptial, and confer with you
Of something nearly that concerns yourselves.

Egeus

With duty and desire we follow you.

Exeunt [all but Lysander and Hermia].

Lysander

How now, my love, why is your cheek so pale?

How chance the roses there do fade so fast?

Hermia

Belike for want of rain, which I could well

Beteem them from the tempest of my eyes.

Lysander

Ay me! For aught that I could ever read,

Could ever hear by tale or history,

The course of true love never did run smooth;

But either it was different in blood—

Hermia

O cross! Too high to be enthralled to low.

Lysander

Or else misgrafted in respect of years—

Hermia

O spite! Too old to be engaged to young.

Lysander

Or else it stood upon the choice of friends—

Hermia

O hell, to choose love by another's eyes!

Lysander

Or if there were a sympathy in choice,

War, death, or sickness did lay siege to it,

Making it momentary as a sound,

Swift as a shadow, short as any dream,

Brief as the lightning in the collied night

That in a spleen unfolds both heaven and earth,

And ere a man hath power to say "Behold!"

The jaws of darkness do devour it up.

So quick bright things come to confusion.

Hermia

If then true lovers have been ever crossed,

It stands as an edict in destiny.
Then let us teach our trial patience,
Because it is a customary cross,
As due to love as thoughts, and dreams, and sighs,
Wishes, and tears, poor fancy's followers.

Lysander

A good persuasion. Therefore, hear me, Hermia:
I have a widow aunt, a dowager
Of great revenue, and she hath no child.
From Athens is her house remote seven leagues;
And she respects me as her only son.
There, gentle Hermia, may I marry thee,
And to that place the sharp Athenian law
Cannot pursue us. If thou lovest me, then,
Steal forth thy father's house tomorrow night;
And in the wood, a league without the town,
Where I did meet thee once with Helena
To do observance to a morn of May,
There will I stay for thee.

Hermia   My good Lysander!

I swear to thee, by Cupid's strongest bow,
By his best arrow with the golden head,
By the simplicity of Venus' doves,
By that which knitteth souls and prospers loves,
And by that fire which burned the Carthage queen
When the false Trojan under sail was seen,
By all the vows that ever men have broke,
In number more than ever women spoke,
In that same place thou hast appointed me
Tomorrow truly will I meet with thee.

Lysander

Keep promise, love. Look, here comes Helena.

Enter Helena.

Hermia

God speed, fair Helena! Whither away?

Helena

    Call you me fair? That "fair" again unsay.
    Demetrius loves your fair. O happy fair!
    Your eyes are lodestars, and your tongue's sweet air
    More tunable than lark to shepherd's ear
    When wheat is green, when hawthorn buds appear.
    Sickness is catching. O, were favor so,
    Yours would I catch, fair Hermia, ere I go;
    My ear should catch your voice, my eye your eye,
    My tongue should catch your tongue's sweet melody.
    Were the world mine, Demetrius being bated,
    The rest I'd give to be to you translated.
    O, teach me how you look and with what art
    You sway the motion of Demetrius' heart.

Hermia

    I frown upon him, yet he loves me still.

Helena

    O, that your frowns would teach my smiles such skill!

Hermia

    I give him curses, yet he gives me love.

Helena

    O, that my prayers could such affection move!

Hermia

    The more I hate, the more he follows me.

Helena

    The more I love, the more he hateth me.

Hermia

    His folly, Helena, is no fault of mine.

Helena

    None, but your beauty. Would that fault were mine!

Hermia

    Take comfort. He no more shall see my face.
    Lysander and myself will fly this place.
    Before the time I did Lysander see
    Seemed Athens as a paradise to me.
    O, then, what graces in my love do dwell,

That he hath turned a heaven unto a hell?

Lysander

Helen, to you our minds we will unfold.
Tomorrow night, when Phoebe doth behold
Her silver visage in the watery glass,
Decking with liquid pearl the bladed grass,
A time that lovers' flights doth still conceal,
Through Athens' gates have we devised to steal.

Hermia

And in the wood, where often you and I
Upon faint primrose beds were wont to lie,
Emptying our bosoms of their counsel sweet,
There my Lysander and myself shall meet,
And thence from Athens turn away our eyes
To seek new friends and stranger companies.
Farewell, sweet playfellow. Pray thou for us,
And good luck grant thee thy Demetrius!
Keep word, Lysander. We must starve our sight
From lovers' food till morrow deep midnight.

Lysander

I will, my Hermia. [*Exit Hermia.*] Helena, adieu.
As you on him, Demetrius dote on you!

[*Exit Lysander.*]

Helena

How happy some o'er other some can be!
Through Athens I am thought as fair as she.
But what of that? Demetrius thinks not so;
He will not know what all but he do know.
And as he errs, doting on Hermia's eyes,
So I, admiring of his qualities.
Things base and vile, holding no quantity,
Love can transpose to form and dignity.
Love looks not with the eyes, but with the mind,
And therefore is winged Cupid painted blind.
Nor hath Love's mind of any judgment taste;
Wings and no eyes figure unheedy haste.

And therefore is Love said to be a child,
Because in choice he is so oft beguiled.
As waggish boys in game themselves forswear,
So the boy Love is perjured everywhere.
For ere Demetrius looked on Hermia's eyne,
He hailed down oaths that he was only mine;
And when this hail some heat from Hermia felt,
So he dissolved, and showers of oaths did melt.
I will go tell him of fair Hermia's flight.
Then to the wood will he tomorrow night
Pursue her; and for this intelligence
If I have thanks, it is a dear expense.
But herein mean I to enrich my pain,
To have his sight thither and back again.   [*Exit.*]

*1.2 ENTER QUINCE THE CARPENTER, AND SNUG THE JOINER, AND
BOTTOM THE WEAVER, AND FLUTE THE BELLOWS MENDER, AND
SNOUT THE TINKER, AND STARVELING THE TAILOR.*

Quince   Is all our company here?

Bottom   You were best to call them generally, man by man, according
to the scrip.

Quince   Here is the scroll of every man's name which is thought fit,
through all Athens, to play in our interlude before the Duke and
the Duchess on his wedding day at night.

Bottom   First, good Peter Quince, say what the play treats on, then
read the names of the actors, and so grow to a point.

Quince   Marry, our play is "The most lamentable comedy and most
cruel death of Pyramus and Thisbe."

Bottom   A very good piece of work, I assure you, and a merry. Now,
good Peter Quince, call forth your actors by the scroll. Masters,
spread yourselves.

Quince   Answer as I call you. Nick Bottom, the weaver.

Bottom   Ready. Name what part I am for, and proceed.

Quince   You, Nick Bottom, are set down for Pyramus.

Bottom   What is Pyramus? A lover or a tyrant?

Quince   A lover, that kills himself most gallant for love.

Bottom   That will ask some tears in the true performing of it. If I
do it, let the audience look to their eyes. I will move storms; I will
condole in some measure. To the rest—yet my chief humor is for a
tyrant. I could play Ercles rarely, or a part to tear a cat in, to make
all split.

"The raging rocks
And shivering shocks
Shall break the locks
     Of prison gates;
And Phibbus' car
Shall shine from far
And make and mar
     The foolish Fates."

This was lofty! Now name the rest of the players. This is Ercles' vein, a tyrant's vein. A lover is more condoling.

Quince   Francis Flute, the bellows mender.

Flute   Here, Peter Quince.

Quince   Flute, you must take Thisbe on you.

Flute   What is Thisbe? A wandering knight?

Quince   It is the lady that Pyramus must love.

Flute   Nay, faith, let not me play a woman. I have a beard coming.

Quince   That's all one. You shall play it in a mask, and you may speak as small as you will.

Bottom   An I may hide my face, let me play Thisbe too. I'll speak in a monstrous little voice: "Thisne, Thisne!" "Ah, Pyramus, my lover dear! Thy Thisbe dear, and lady dear!"

Quince   No, no, you must play Pyramus, and Flute, you Thisbe.

Bottom   Well, proceed.

Quince   Robin Starveling, the tailor.

Starveling   Here, Peter Quince.

Quince   Robin Starveling, you must play Thisbe's mother. Tom Snout, the tinker.

Snout   Here, Peter Quince.

Quince   You, Pyramus' father; myself, Thisbe's father; Snug, the joiner, you, the lion's part; and I hope here is a play fitted.

Snug   Have you the lion's part written? Pray you, if it be, give it me, for I am slow of study.

Quince   You may do it extempore, for it is nothing but roaring.

Bottom   Let me play the lion too. I will roar that I will do any man's heart good to hear me. I will roar that I will make the Duke say, "Let him roar again, let him roar again."

Quince   An you should do it too terribly, you would fright the
      Duchess and the ladies, that they would shriek; and that were
      enough to hang us all.

All   That would hang us, every mother's son.

Bottom   I grant you, friends, if you should fright the ladies out of
      their wits, they would have no more discretion but to hang us; but
      I will aggravate my voice so that I will roar you as gently as any
      sucking dove; I will roar you an 'twere any nightingale.

Quince   You can play no part but Pyramus; for Pyramus is a sweet-
      faced man, a proper man as one shall see in a summer's day, a
      most lovely gentlemanlike man. Therefore you must needs play
      Pyramus.

Bottom   Well, I will undertake it. What beard were I best to play it
      in?

Quince   Why, what you will.

Bottom   I will discharge it in either your straw-color beard, your
      orange-tawny beard, your purple-in-grain beard, or your French-
      crown-color beard, your perfect yellow.

Quince   Some of your French crowns have no hair at all, and then
      you will play barefaced. But, masters, here are your parts. [*He distrib-
      utes parts.*] And I am to entreat you, request you, and desire you to
      con them by tomorrow night, and meet me in the palace wood, a
      mile without the town, by moonlight. There will we rehearse; for if
      we meet in the city, we shall be dogged with company, and our de-
      vices known. In the meantime I will draw a bill of properties, such
      as our play wants. I pray you, fail me not.

Bottom   We will meet, and there we may rehearse most obscenely and
      courageously. Take pains, be perfect. Adieu.

Quince   At the Duke's oak we meet.

Bottom   Enough. Hold, or cut bowstrings.   [*Exeunt.*]

2.1 ENTER A FAIRY AT ONE DOOR, AND
ROBIN GOODFELLOW [PUCK] AT ANOTHER.

Puck
    How now, spirit, whither wander you?

Fairy

> Over hill, over dale,
>> Through bush, through brier,
> Over park, over pale,
>> Through flood, through fire,
> I do wander everywhere.
> Swifter than the moon's sphere;
> And I serve the Fairy Queen,
> To dew her orbs upon the green.
> The cowslips tall her pensioners be.
> In their gold coats spots you see;
> Those be rubies, fairy favors;
> In those freckles live their savors.

I must go seek some dewdrops here
And hang a pearl in every cowslip's ear.
Farewell, thou lob of spirits; I'll be gone.
Our Queen and all her elves come here anon.

Puck

The King doth keep his revels here tonight.
Take heed the Queen come not within his sight.
For Oberon is passing fell and wrath,
Because that she as her attendant hath
A lovely boy, stolen from an Indian king;
She never had so sweet a changeling.
And jealous Oberon would have the child
Knight of his train, to trace the forests wild.
But she perforce withholds me lovèd boy,
Crowns him with flowers, and makes him all her joy.
And now they never meet in grove or green,
By fountain clear, or spangled starlight sheen,
But they do square, that all their elves for fear
Creep into acorn cups and hide them there.

Fairy

Either I mistake your shape and making quite,
Or else you are that shrewd and knavish sprite
Called Robin Goodfellow. Are not you he

That frights the maidens of the villagery,
Skim milk, and sometimes labor in the quern,
And bootless make the breathless huswife churn,
And sometimes make the drink to bear no barm,
Mislead night wanderers, laughing at their harm?
Those that "Hobgoblin" call you, and "Sweet Puck,"
You do their work, and they shall have good luck.
Are you not he?
Puck   Thou speakest aright;
I am that merry wanderer of the night.
I jest to Oberon and make him smile
When I a fat and bean-fed horse beguile,
Neighing in likeness of a filly foal;
And sometimes lurk I in a gossip's bowl
In very likeness of a roasted crab,
And when she drinks, against her lips I bob
And on her withered dewlap pour the ale.

The wisest aunt, telling the saddest tale,
Sometimes for three-foot stool mistaketh me;
Then slip I from her bum, down topples she,
And "Tailor" cries, and falls into a cough;
And then the whole choir hold their hips and laugh,
And waxen in their mirth, and neeze, and swear
A merrier hour was never wasted there.
But, room, fairy! Here comes Oberon.

Fairy

And here my mistress. Would that he were gone!

*Enter [Oberon] the King of Fairies at one door, with his train,
and [Titania] the Queen at another, with hers.*

Oberon

Ill met by moonlight, proud Titania.

Titania

What, jealous Oberon? Fairies, skip hence.
I have forsworn his bed and company.

Oberon

Tarry, rash wanton. Am not I thy lord?

Titania

Then I must be thy lady; but I know
When thou hast stolen away from Fairyland
And in the shape of Corin sat all day,
Playing on pipes of corn and versing love
To amorous Phillida. Why art thou here
Come from the farthest step of India,
But that, forsooth, the bouncing Amazon,
Your buskined mistress and your warrior love,
To Theseus must be wedded, and you come
To give their bed joy and prosperity.

Oberon

How canst thou thus for shame, Titania,
Glance at my credit with Hippolyta,
Knowing I know thy love to Theseus?
Didst not thou lead him through the glimmering night

From Perigenia, whom he ravishèd?
And make him with fair Aegles break his faith,
With Ariadne and Antiopa?

Titania

These are the forgeries of jealousy;
And never, since the middle summer's spring,
Met we on hill, in dale, forest, or mead,
By pavèd fountain or by rushy brook,
Or in the beachèd margent of the sea,
To dance our ringlets to the whistling wind,
But with thy brawls thou hast disturbed our sport.
Therefore the winds, piping to us in vain,
As in revenge, have sucked up from the sea
Contagious fogs which, falling in the land,
Hath every pelting river made so proud
That they have overborne their continents.
The ox hath therefore stretched his yoke in vain,
The plowman lost his sweat, and the green corn
Hath rotted ere his youth attained a beard;
The fold stands empty in the drownèd field,
And crows are fatted with the murrain flock;
The nine-men's morris is filled up with mud,
And the quaint mazes in the wanton green
For lack of tread are undistinguishable.
The human mortals want their winter here;
No night is now with hymn or carol blessed.
Therefore the moon, the governess of floods,
Pale in her anger, washes all the air,
That rheumatic diseases do abound.
And thorough this distemperature we see
The seasons alter: hoary-headed frosts
Fall in the fresh lap of the crimson rose,
And on old Hiems' thin and icy crown
An odorous chaplet of sweet summer buds
Is, as in mockery, set. The spring, the summer,
The childing autumn, angry winter, change

Their wonted liveries, and me mazèd world
By their increase now knows not which is which.
And this same progeny of evils comes
From our debate, from our dissension.
We are their parents and original.

Oberon

Do you amend it, then. It lies in you.
Why should Titania cross her Oberon?
I do but beg a little changeling boy
To be my henchman.

Titania   Set your heart at rest.
The fairy land buys not the child of me.
His mother was a vot'ress of my order,
And in the spicèd Indian air by night
Full often hath she gossiped by my side
And sat with me on Neptune's yellow sands,
Marking th' embarkèd traders on the flood,
When we have laughed to see the sails conceive
And grow big-bellied with the wanton wind;
Which she, with pretty and with swimming gait,
Following—her womb then rich with my young squire—

Would imitate, and sail upon the land
To fetch me trifles, and return again
As from a voyage, rich with merchandise.
But she, being mortal, of that boy did die;
And for her sake do I rear up her boy,
And for her sake I will not part with him.

Oberon

How long within this wood intend you stay?

Titania

Perchance till after Theseus' wedding day.
If you will patiently dance in our round
And see our moonlight revels, go with us;
If not, shun me, and I will spare your haunts.

Oberon

Give me that boy, and I will go with thee.

Titania

Not for thy fairy kingdom. Fairies, away!
We shall chide downright, if I longer stay.

Exeunt [Titania with her train].

Oberon

Well, go thy way. Thou shalt not from this grove
Till I torment thee for this injury.

My gentle Puck, come hither. Thou rememb'rest
Since once I sat upon a promontory,
And heard a mermaid on a dolphin's back
Uttering such dulcet and harmonious breath
That the rude sea grew civil at her song,
And certain stars shot madly from their spheres
To hear the sea-maid's music?

Puck   I remember.

Oberon

That very time I saw, but thou couldst not,
Flying between the cold moon and the earth
Cupid, all armed. A certain aim he took
At a fair vestal thronèd by the west,
And loosed his love shaft smartly from his bow
As it should pierce a hundred thousand hearts;
But I might see young Cupid's fiery shaft
Quenched in the chaste beams of the watery moon,
And the imperial vot'ress passèd on,
In maiden meditation, fancy-free.
Yet marked I where the bolt of Cupid fell:
It fell upon a little western flower,
Before milk-white, now purple with love's wound,
And maidens call it love-in-idleness.
Fetch me that flower; the herb I showed thee once.
The juice of it on sleeping eyelids laid
Will make or man or woman madly dote
Upon the next live creature that it sees.
Fetch me this herb, and be thou here again
Ere the leviathan can swim a league.

Puck

I'll put a girdle round about the earth
In forty minutes.   [*Exit.*]

Oberon   Having once this juice,
I'll watch Titania when she is asleep
And drop the liquor of it in her eyes.
The next thing then she waking looks upon,

Be it on lion, bear, or wolf, or bull,
On meddling monkey, or on busy ape,
She shall pursue it with the soul of love.
And ere I take this charm from off her sight,
As I can take it with another herb,
I'll make her render up her page to me.
But who comes here? I am invisible,
And I will overhear their conference.

Enter Demetrius, Helena following him.

Demetrius
I love thee not; therefore pursue me not.
Where is Lysander and fair Hermia?
The one I'll slay; the other slayeth me.
Thou toldst me they were stol'n unto this wood;

And here am I, and wood within this wood
Because I cannot meet my Hermia.
Hence, get thee gone, and follow me no more.

Helena

You draw me, you hardhearted adamant!
But yet you draw not iron, for my heart
Is true as steel. Leave you your power to draw,
And I shall have no power to follow you.

Demetrius

Do I entice you? Do I speak you fair?
Or rather do I not in plainest truth
Tell you I do not nor I cannot love you?

Helena

And even for that do I love you the more.
I am your spaniel; and, Demetrius,
The more you beat me I will fawn on you.
Use me but as your spaniel, spurn me, strike me,
Neglect me, lose me; only give me leave,
Unworthy as I am, to follow you.
What worser place can I beg in your love—
And yet a place of high respect with me—
Than to be usèd as you use your dog?

Demetrius

Tempt not too much the hatred of my spirit,
For I am sick when I do look on thee.

Helena

And I am sick when I look not on you.

Demetrius

You do impeach your modesty too much
To leave the city and commit yourself
Into the hands of one that loves you not,
To trust the opportunity of night
And the ill counsel of a desert place
With the rich worth of your virginity.

Helena

Your virtue is my privilege. For that

It is not night when I do see your face,
Therefore I think I am not in the night;
Nor doth this wood lack worlds of company,
For you, in my respect, are all the world.
Then how can it be said I am alone
When all the world is here to look on me?

Demetrius

I'll run from thee and hide me in the brakes,
And leave thee to the mercy of wild beasts.

Helena

The wildest hath not such a heart as you.
Run when you will. The story shall be changed:
Apollo flies and Daphne holds the chase,
The dove pursues the griffin, the mild hind
Makes speed to catch the tiger—bootless speed,
When cowardice pursues and valor flies!

Demetrius

I will not stay thy questions. Let me go!
Or if thou follow me, do not believe
But I shall do thee mischief in the wood.

Helena

Ay, in the temple, in the town, the field,
You do me mischief. Fie, Demetrius!
Your wrongs do set a scandal on my sex.
We cannot fight for love, as men may do;
We should be wooed and were not made to woo.

[*Exit Demetrius.*]

I'll follow thee and make a heaven of hell,
To die upon the hand I love so well.   [*Exit.*]

Oberon

Fare thee well, nymph. Ere he do leave this grove
Thou shalt fly him, and he shall seek thy love.

Enter Puck.

Hast thou the flower there? Welcome, wanderer.

Puck

Ay, there it is.   [*He offers the flower.*]

Oberon   I pray thee, give it me.

I know a bank where the wild thyme blows,
Where oxlips and the nodding violet grows,
Quite overcanopied with luscious woodbine,
With sweet muskroses and with eglantine.
There sleeps Titania sometime of the night,
Lulled in these flowers with dances and delight;
And there the snake throws her enameled skin,
Weed wide enough to wrap a fairy in.
And with the juice of this I'll streak her eyes
And make her full of hateful fantasies.
Take thou some of it, and seek through this grove.

[*He gives some love juice.*]

A sweet Athenian lady is in love
With a disdainful youth. Anoint his eyes,
But do it when the next thing he espies
May be the lady. Thou shalt know the man
By the Athenian garments he hath on.
Effect it with some care, that he may prove
More fond on her than she upon her love;
And look thou meet me ere the first cock crow.

Puck

Fear not, my lord, your servant shall do so.

Exeunt [separately].

2.2 ENTER TITANIA, QUEEN OF FAIRIES, WITH HER TRAIN.

Titania

Come, now a roundel and a fairy song;
Then, for the third part of a minute, hence—
Some to kill cankers in the muskrose buds,
Some war with reremice for their leathern wings
To make my small elves coats, and some keep back

The clamorous owl, that nightly hoots and wonders
At our quaint spirits. Sing me now asleep.
Then to your offices, and let me rest.

Fairies sing.

First Fairy

You spotted snakes with double tongue,
Thorny hedgehogs, be not seen;
Newts and blindworms, do no wrong;
Come not near our Fairy Queen.

Chorus [*dancing*]

Philomel, with melody
Sing in our sweet lullaby;
Lulla, lulla, lullaby, lulla, lulla, lullaby.
Never harm
Nor spell nor charm
Come our lovely lady nigh.
So good night, with lullaby.

First Fairy

Weaving spiders, come not here;
Hence, you long-legged spinners, hence!
Beetles black, approach not near;
Worm nor snail, do no offense.

Chorus [*dancing*]

Philomel, with melody
Sing in our sweet lullaby;
Lulla, lulla, lullaby, lulla, lulla, lullaby.
Never harm
Nor spell nor charm
Come our lovely lady nigh.
So good night, with lullaby.

[*Titania sleeps.*]

Second Fairy

Hence, away! Now all is well.
One aloof stand sentinel.

[*Exeunt Fairies, leaving one sentinel.*]

Enter Oberon [and squeezes the flower on Titania's eyelids].

Oberon

 What thou seest when thou dost wake,
 Do it for thy true love take;
 Love and languish for his sake.
 Be it ounce, or cat, or bear,
 Pard, or boar with bristled hair,
 In thy eye that shall appear
 When thou wak'st, it is thy dear.
 Wake when some vile thing is near.   [*Exit.*]

Enter Lysander and Hermia.

Lysander

Fair love, you faint with wandering in the wood;
 And to speak truth, I have forgot our way.
We'll rest us, Hermia, if you think it good,
 And tarry for the comfort of the day.

Hermia

Be it so, Lysander. Find you out a bed,
For I upon this bank will rest my head.

Lysander

One turf shall serve as pillow for us both;
One heart, one bed, two bosoms, and one troth.

Hermia

Nay, good Lysander, for my sake, my dear,
Lie further off yet. Do not lie so near.

Lysander

O, take the sense, sweet, of my innocence!
Love takes the meaning in love's conference.
I mean that my heart unto yours is knit,
So that but one heart we can make of it;
Two bosoms interchainèd with an oath—
So then two bosoms and a single troth.
Then by your side no bed-room me deny,
For lying so, Hermia, I do not lie.

Hermia

Lysander riddles very prettily.
Now much beshrew my manners and my pride
If Hermia meant to say Lysander lied.
But, gentle friend, for love and courtesy
Lie further off, in human modesty.
Such separation as may well be said
Becomes a virtuous bachelor and a maid,
So far be distant, and, good night, sweet friend.
Thy love ne'er alter till thy sweet life end!

Lysander

Amen, amen, to that fair prayer, say I,
And then end life when I end loyalty!
Here is my bed. Sleep give thee all his rest!

Hermia

With half that wish the wisher's eyes be pressed!

[*They sleep, separated by a short distance.*]

Enter Puck.

Puck

Through the forest have I gone,

But Athenian found I none
On whose eyes I might approve
This flower's force in stirring love.
Night and silence.—Who is here?
Weeds of Athens he doth wear.
This is he, my master said,
Despisèd the Athenian maid;
And here the maiden, sleeping sound,
On the dank and dirty ground.
Pretty soul, she durst not lie
Near this lack-love, this kill-courtesy.
Churl, upon thy eyes I throw
All the power this charm doth owe.

[*He applies the love juice.*]

When thou wak'st, let love forbid
Sleep his seat on thy eyelid.
So awake when I am gone,
For I must now to Oberon.   [*Exit.*]

Enter Demetrius and Helena, running.

Helena
Stay, though thou kill me, sweet Demetrius!
Demetrius
I charge thee, hence, and do not haunt me thus.
Helena
O, wilt thou darkling leave me? Do not so.
Demetrius
Stay, on thy peril! I alone will go.   [*Exit.*]
Helena
O, I am out of breath in this fond chase!
The more my prayer, the lesser is my grace.
Happy is Hermia, wheresoe'er she lies,
For she hath blessèd and attractive eyes.
How came her eyes so bright? Not with salt tears;
If so, my eyes are oftener washed than hers.
No, no, I am as ugly as a bear,

For beasts that meet me run away for fear.
Therefore no marvel though Demetrius
Do, as a monster, fly my presence thus.
What wicked and dissembling glass of mine
Made me compare with Hermia's sphery eyne?
But who is here? Lysander, on the ground?
Dead, or asleep? I see no blood, no wound.
Lysander, if you live, good sir, awake.

Lysander [*awaking*]

And run through fire I will for thy sweet sake.
Transparent Helena! Nature shows art,
That through thy bosom makes me see thy heart.
Where is Demetrius? O, how fit a word
Is that vile name to perish on my sword!

Helena

Do not say so, Lysander; say not so.
What though he love your Hermia? Lord, what though?
Yet Hermia still loves you. Then be content.

Lysander

Content with Hermia? No! I do repent
The tedious minutes I with her have spent.
Not Hermia but Helena I love.
Who will not change a raven for a dove?
The will of man is by his reason swayed,
And reason says you are the worthier maid.
Things growing are not ripe until their season;
So I, being young, till now ripe not to reason.
And, touching now the point of human skill,
Reason becomes the marshal to my will
And leads me to your eyes, where I o'erlook
Love's stories written in love's richest book.

Helena

Wherefore was I to this keen mockery born?
When at your hands did I deserve this scorn?
Is 't not enough, is 't not enough, young man,

That I did never—no, nor never can—
Deserve a sweet look from Demetrius' eye,
But you must flout my insufficiency?
Good troth, you do me wrong, good sooth, you do,
In such disdainful manner me to woo.
But fare you well. Perforce I must confess
I thought you lord of more true gentleness.
O, that a lady, of one man refused,
Should of another therefore be abused!   [Exit.]

Lysander

She sees not Hermia. Hermia, sleep thou there,
And never mayst thou come Lysander near!
For as a surfeit of the sweetest things
The deepest loathing to the stomach brings,
Or as the heresies that men do leave
Are hated most of those they did deceive,
So thou, my surfeit and my heresy,
Of all be hated, but the most of me!
And, all my powers, address your love and might
To honor Helen and to be her knight!   [Exit.]

Hermia [awaking]

Help me, Lysander, help me! Do thy best
To pluck this crawling serpent from my breast!
Ay me, for pity! What a dream was here!
Lysander, look how I do quake with fear.
Methought a serpent ate my heart away,
And you sat smiling at his cruel prey.
Lysander! What, removed? Lysander! Lord!
What, out of hearing? Gone? No sound, no word?
Alack, where are you? Speak, an if you hear;
Speak, of all loves! I swoon almost with fear.
No? Then I well perceive you are not nigh.
Either death, or you, I'll find immediately.

                              Exit. [The sleeping Titania remains.]

3.1 ENTER THE CLOWNS [QUINCE, SNUG, BOTTOM, FLUTE,
SNOUT, AND STARVELING].

Bottom   Are we all met?

Quince   Pat, pat; and here's a marvelous convenient place for our re-
hearsal. This green plot shall be our stage, this hawthorn brake our
tiring-house, and we will do it in action as we will do it before the
Duke.

Bottom   Peter Quince?

Quince   What sayest thou, bully Bottom?

Bottom   There are things in this comedy of Pyramus and Thisbe that
will never please. First, Pyramus must draw a sword to kill himself,
which the ladies cannot abide. How answer you that?

Snout   By 'r lakin, a parlous fear.

Starveling   I believe we must leave the killing out, when all is done.

Bottom   Not a whit. I have a device to make all well. Write me a prologue, and let the prologue seem to say, we will do no harm with
our swords, and that Pyramus is not killed indeed; and for the
more better assurance, tell them that I, Pyramus, am not Pyramus
but Bottom the weaver. This will put them out of fear.

Quince   Well, we will have such a prologue, and it shall be written in
eight and six.

Bottom   No, make it two more: let it be written in eight and eight.

Snout   Will not the ladies be afeard of the lion?

Starveling   I fear it, I promise you.

Bottom   Masters, you ought to consider with yourself, to bring in—
God shield us!—a lion among ladies is a most dreadful thing. For
there is not a more fearful wildfowl than your lion living, and we
ought to look to 't.

Snout   Therefore another prologue must tell he is not a lion.

Bottom   Nay, you must name his name, and half his face must be
seen through the lion's neck, and he himself must speak through,
saying thus or to the same defect: "Ladies," or "Fair ladies, I would
wish you," or "I would request you," or "I would entreat you, not to
fear, not to tremble; my life for yours. If you think I come hither as
a lion, it were pity of my life. No, I am no such thing; I am a man as

other men are." And there indeed let him name his name, and tell them plainly he is Snug the joiner.

Quince   Well, it shall be so. But there is two hard things: that is, to bring me moonlight into a chamber; for, you know, Pyramus and Thisbe meet by moonlight.

Snout   Doth the moon shine that night we play our play?

Bottom   A calendar, a calendar! Look in the almanac. Find out moonshine, find out moonshine.

[*They consult an almanac.*]

Quince   Yes, it doth shine that night.

Bottom   Why then may you leave a casement of the great chamber window where we play open, and the moon may shine in at the casement.

Quince   Ay; or else one must come in with a bush of thorns and a lantern and say he comes to disfigure, or to present, the person of Moonshine. Then there is another thing: we must have a wall in the great chamber; for Pyramus and Thisbe, says the story, did talk through the chink of a wall.

Snout   You can never bring in a wall. What say you, Bottom?

Bottom   Some man or other must present Wall. And let him have some plaster, or some loam, or some roughcast about him, to signify wall; or let him hold his fingers thus, and through that cranny shall Pyramus and Thisbe whisper.

Quince   If that may be, then all is well. Come, sit down, every mother's son, and rehearse your parts. Pyramus, you begin. When you have spoken your speech, enter into that brake, and so everyone according to his cue.

Enter Robin [Puck].

Puck [*aside*]
What hempen homespuns have we swaggering here
So near the cradle of the Fairy Queen?
What, a play toward? I'll be an auditor;
An actor, too, perhaps, if I see cause.

Quince   Speak, Pyramus. Thisbe, stand forth.

Bottom [*as Pyramus*]
"Thisbe, the flowers of odious savors sweet—"

Quince   Odors, odors.

Bottom   "—Odors savors sweet;
    So hath thy breath, my dearest Thisbe dear.
But hark, a voice! Stay thou but here awhile,
    And by and by I will to thee appear."   [*Exit.*]

Puck
A stranger Pyramus than e'er played here.   [*Exit.*]

Flute   Must I speak now?

Quince   Ay, marry, must you; for you must understand he goes but to see a noise that he heard, and is to come again.

Flute [*as Thisbe*]
"Most radiant Pyramus, most lily-white of hue,
    Of color like the red rose on triumphant brier,
Most brisky juvenal and eke most lovely Jew,
    As true as truest horse that yet would never tire.
I'll meet thee, Pyramus, at Ninny's tomb."

Quince   "Ninus' tomb," man. Why, you must not speak that yet. That you answer to Pyramus. You speak all your part at once, cues and all. Pyramus, enter. Your cue is past; it is "never tire."

Flute

O—"As true as truest horse, that yet would never tire."

Enter Puck, and Bottom as Pyramus with the ass head.

Bottom

"If I were fair, Thisbe, I were only thine."

Quince   O, monstrous! O, strange! We are haunted. Pray, masters! Fly, masters! Help!

[Exeunt Quince, Snug, Flute, Snout, and Starveling.]

Puck

I'll follow you, I'll lead you about a round,
    Through bog, through bush, through brake, through brier.
Sometimes a horse I'll be, sometimes a hound,
    A hog, a headless bear, sometimes a fire;
And neigh, and bark, and grunt, and roar, and burn,
Like horse, hound, hog, bear, fire, at every turn.   *[Exit.]*

Bottom   Why do they run away? This is a knavery of them to make me afeard.

Enter Snout.

Snout   O Bottom, thou art changed! What do I see on thee?

Bottom   What do you see? You see an ass head of your own, do you?

[Exit Snout.]

Enter Quince.

Quince   Bless thee, Bottom, bless thee! Thou art translated.   *[Exit.]*

Bottom   I see their knavery. This is to make an ass of me, to fright me, if they could. But I will not stir from this place, do what they can. I will walk up and down here, and will sing, that they shall hear I am not afraid.   *[He sings.]*

The ouzel cock so black of hue,
    With orange-tawny bill,
The throstle with his note so true,
    The wren with little quill—

Titania [*awaking*]

What angel wakes me from my flowery bed?

Bottom [*sings*]
>   The finch, the sparrow, and the lark,
>   The plainsong cuckoo gray,
>   Whose note full many a man doth mark,
>   And dares not answer nay—

For indeed, who would set his wit to so foolish a bird? Who would
give a bird the lie, though he cry "cuckoo" never so?

Titania
>   I pray thee, gentle mortal, sing again.
>   Mine ear is much enamored of thy note;
>   So is mine eye enthrallèd to thy shape;
>   And thy fair virtue's force perforce doth move me
>   On the first view to say, to swear, I love thee.

Bottom   Methinks, mistress, you should have little reason for that.
And yet, to say the truth, reason and love keep little company together nowadays—the more the pity that some honest neighbors
will not make them friends. Nay, I can gleek upon occasion.

Titania

    Thou art as wise as thou art beautiful.

Bottom   Not so, neither. But if I had wit enough to get out of this wood, I have enough to serve mine own turn.

Titania

    Out of this wood do not desire to go.

    Thou shalt remain here, whether thou wilt or no.

    I am a spirit of no common rate.

    The summer still doth tend upon my state,

    And I do love thee. Therefore, go with me.

    I'll give thee fairies to attend on thee,

    And they shall fetch thee jewels from the deep,

    And sing while thou on pressèd flowers dost sleep.

    And I will purge thy mortal grossness so

    That thou shalt like an airy spirit go.

    Peaseblossom, Cobweb, Mote, and Mustardseed!

Enter four Fairies [Peaseblossom, Cobweb, Mote, and Mustardseed].

Peaseblossom   Ready.

Cobweb

    And I.

Mote   And I.

Mustardseed   And I.

All   Where shall we go?

Titania

    Be kind and courteous to this gentleman.

    Hop in his walks and gambol in his eyes;

    Feed him with apricots and dewberries,

    With purple grapes, green figs, and mulberries;

    The honey bags steal from the humble-bees,

    And for night tapers crop their waxen thighs

    And light them at the fiery glowworms' eyes,

    To have my love to bed and to arise;

    And pluck the wings from painted butterflies

    To fan the moonbeams from his sleeping eyes.

Nod to him, elves, and do him courtesies.

Peaseblossom   Hail, mortal!

Cobweb   Hail!

Mote   Hail!

Mustardseed   Hail!

Bottom   I cry your worships mercy, heartily. I beseech your worship's name.

Cobweb   Cobweb.

Bottom   I shall desire you of more acquaintance, good Master Cobweb. If I cut my finger, I shall make bold with you.—Your name, honest gentleman?

Peaseblossom   Peaseblossom.

Bottom   I pray you, commend me to Mistress Squash, your mother, and to Master Peascod, your father. Good Master Peaseblossom, I shall desire you of more acquaintance too.—Your name, I beseech you, sir?

Mustardseed   Mustardseed.

Bottom   Good Master Mustardseed, I know your patience well. That same cowardly, giantlike ox-beef hath devoured many a gentleman of your house. I promise you, your kindred hath made my eyes water ere now. I desire you of more acquaintance, good Master Mustardseed.

Titania

Come wait upon him; lead him to my bower.
    The moon methinks looks with a watery eye;
And when she weeps, weeps every little flower,
Lamenting some enforcèd chastity.
Tie up my lover's tongue; bring him silently.   [*Exeunt.*]

3.2 ENTER [OBERON,] KING OF FAIRIES.

Oberon

I wonder if Titania be awaked;
Then, what it was that next came in her eye,
Which she must dote on in extremity.

[*Enter*] *Robin Goodfellow* [*Puck*].

Here comes my messenger. How now, mad spirit?
What night-rule now about this haunted grove?
Puck
My mistress with a monster is in love.
Near to her close and consecrated bower,
While she was in her dull and sleeping hour,
A crew of patches, rude mechanicals,
That work for bread upon Athenian stalls,
Were met together to rehearse a play
Intended for great Theseus' nuptial day.
The shallowest thickskin of that barren sort,
Who Pyramus presented, in their sport
Forsook his scene and entered in a brake.
When I did him at this advantage take,
An ass's noll I fixèd on his head.

Anon his Thisbe must be answerèd,
And forth my mimic comes. When they him spy,
As wild geese that the creeping fowler eye,
Or russet-pated choughs, many in sort,
Rising and cawing at the gun's report,
Sever themselves and madly sweep the sky,
So, at his sight, away his fellows fly;
And, at our stamp, here o'er and o'er one falls;
He "Murder!" cries and help from Athens calls.
Their sense thus weak, lost with their fears thus strong,
Made senseless things begin to do them wrong,
For briers and thorns at their apparel snatch;
Some, sleeves—some, hats; from yielders all things catch.
I led them on in this distracted fear
And left sweet Pyramus translated there,
When in that moment, so it came to pass,
Titania waked and straightway loved an ass.

Oberon
This falls out better than I could devise.
But hast thou yet latched the Athenian's eyes
With the love juice, as I did bid thee do?

Puck
I took him sleeping—that is finished too—
And the Athenian woman by his side,
That, when he waked, of force she must be eyed.

Enter Demetrius and Hermia.

Oberon
Stand close. This is the same Athenian.

Puck
This is the woman, but not this the man.

[They stand aside.]

Demetrius
O, why rebuke you him that loves you so?
Lay breath so bitter on your bitter foe.

Hermia

    Now I but chide; but I should use thee worse,
    For thou, I fear, hast given me cause to curse.
    If thou hast slain Lysander in his sleep,
    Being o'er shoes in blood, plunge in the deep,
    And kill me too.
    The sun was not so true unto the day
    As he to me. Would he have stolen away
    From sleeping Hermia? I'll believe as soon
    This whole earth may be bored, and that the moon
    May through the center creep, and so displease
    Her brother's noontide with th' Antipodes.
    It cannot be but thou hast murdered him;
    So should a murderer look, so dead, so grim.

Demetrius

    So should the murdered look, and so should I,
    Pierced through the heart with your stern cruelty.
    Yet you, the murderer, look as bright, as clear
    As yonder Venus in her glimmering sphere.

Hermia

What's this to my Lysander? Where is he?
Ah, good Demetrius, wilt thou give him me?

Demetrius

I had rather give his carcass to my hounds.

Hermia

Out, dog! Out, cur! Thou driv'st me past the bounds
Of maiden's patience. Hast thou slain him, then?
Henceforth be never numbered among men.
O, once tell true, tell true, even for my sake:
Durst thou have looked upon him being awake?
And hast thou killed him sleeping? O brave touch!
Could not a worm, an adder, do so much?
An adder did it; for with doubler tongue
Than thine, thou serpent, never adder stung.

Demetrius

You spend your passion on a misprised mood.
I am not guilty of Lysander's blood,
Nor is he dead, for aught that I can tell.

Hermia

I pray thee, tell me then that he is well.

Demetrius

And if I could, what should I get therefor?

Hermia

A privilege never to see me more.
And from thy hated presence part I so.
See me no more, whether he be dead or no.   [*Exit.*]

Demetrius

There is no following her in this fierce vein.
Here therefore for a while I will remain.
So sorrow's heaviness doth heavier grow
For debt that bankrupt sleep doth sorrow owe,
Which now in some slight measure it will pay,
If for his tender here I make some stay.

                                   [*He*] *lie*[*s*] *down* [*and sleeps*].

Oberon

> What hast thou done? Thou hast mistaken quite
> And laid the love juice on some true love's sight.
> Of thy misprision must perforce ensue
> Some true love turned, and not a false turned true.

Puck

> Then fate o'errules, that, one man holding troth,
> A million fail, confounding oath on oath.

Oberon

> About the wood go swifter than the wind,
> And Helena of Athens look thou find.
> All fancy-sick she is and pale of cheer
> With sighs of love, that cost the fresh blood dear.
> By some illusion see thou bring her here.
> I'll charm his eyes against she do appear.

Puck

> I go, I go, look how I go,
> Swifter than arrow from the Tartar's bow.   [*Exit.*]

Oberon [*applying love juice to Demetrius' eyes*]

> Flower of this purple dye,

Hit with Cupid's archery,
Sink in apple of his eye.
When his love he doth espy,
Let her shine as gloriously
As the Venus of the sky.
When thou wak'st, if she be by,
Beg of her for remedy.

Enter Puck.

Puck

Captain of our fairy band,
Helena is here at hand,
And the youth, mistook by me,
Pleading for a lover's fee.
Shall we their fond pageant see?
Lord, what fools these mortals be!

Oberon

Stand aside. The noise they make
Will cause Demetrius to awake.

Puck

Then will two at once woo one;
That must needs be sport alone.
And those things do best please me
That befall preposterously.

[*They stand aside.*]

Enter Lysander and Helena.

Lysander

Why should you think that I should woo in scorn?
    Scorn and derision never come in tears.
Look when I vow, I weep; and vows so born,
    In their nativity all truth appears.
How can these things in me seem scorn to you,
Bearing the badge of faith to prove them true?

Helena

You do advance your cunning more and more.
    When truth kills truth, O, devilish-holy fray!

These vows are Hermia's. Will you give her o'er?
    Weigh oath with oath, and you will nothing weigh.
Your vows to her and me, put in two scales,
Will even weigh, and both as light as tales.
Lysander
I had no judgment when to her I swore.
Helena
Nor none, in my mind, now you give her o'er.
Lysander
Demetrius loves her, and he loves not you.
Demetrius [*awaking*]
O Helen, goddess, nymph, perfect, divine!
To what, my love, shall I compare thine eyne?
Crystal is muddy. O, how ripe in show
Thy lips, those kissing cherries, tempting grow!
That pure congealèd white, high Taurus' snow,
Fanned with the eastern wind, turns to a crow
When thou hold'st up thy hand. O, let me kiss
This princess of pure white, this seal of bliss!
Helena
O spite! O hell! I see you all are bent
To set against me for your merriment,
If you were civil and knew courtesy,
You would not do me thus much injury.
Can you not hate me, as I know you do,
But you must join in souls to mock me too?
If you were men, as men you are in show,
You would not use a gentle lady so—
To vow, and swear, and superpraise my parts,
When I am sure you hate me with your hearts.
You both are rivals, and love Hermia,
And now both rivals to mock Helena.
A trim exploit, a manly enterprise,
To conjure tears up in a poor maid's eyes
With your derision! None of noble sort
Would so offend a virgin and extort

A poor soul's patience, all to make you sport.
Lysander
    You are unkind, Demetrius. Be not so.
    For you love Hermia; this you know I know.
    And here, with all good will, with all my heart,
    In Hermia's love I yield you up my part;
    And yours of Helena to me bequeath,
    Whom I do love, and will do till my death.
Helena
    Never did mockers waste more idle breath.
Demetrius
    Lysander, keep thy Hermia; I will none.
    If e'er I loved her, all that love is gone.
    My heart to her but as guestwise sojourned,
    And now to Helen is it home returned,
    There to remain.
Lysander   Helen, it is not so.

Demetrius

    Disparage not the faith thou dost not know,
    Lest, to thy peril, thou aby it dear.
    Look where thy love comes; yonder is thy dear.

Enter Hermia.

Hermia

    Dark night, that from the eye his function takes,
    The ear more quick of apprehension makes;
    Wherein it doth impair the seeing sense,
    It pays the hearing double recompense.
    Thou art not by mine eye, Lysander, found;
    Mine ear, I thank it, brought me to thy sound.
    But why unkindly didst thou leave me so?

Lysander

    Why should he stay, whom love doth press to go?

Hermia

    What love could press Lysander from my side?

Lysander

    Lysander's love, that would not let him bide—
    Fair Helena, who more engilds the night
    Than all yon fiery oes and eyes of light.
    Why seek'st thou me? Could not this make thee know
    The hate I bear thee made me leave thee so?

Hermia

    You speak not as you think. It cannot be.

Helena

    Lo, she is one of this confederacy!
    Now I perceive they have conjoined all three
    To fashion this false sport, in spite of me.
    Injurious Hermia, most ungrateful maid!
    Have you conspired, have you with these contrived
    To bait me with this foul derision?
    Is all the counsel that we two have shared—
    The sisters' vows, the hours that we have spent
    When we have chid the hasty-footed time

For parting us—O, is all forgot?
All schooldays' friendship, childhood innocence?
We, Hermia, like two artificial gods
Have with our needles created both one flower,
Both on one sampler, sitting on one cushion,
Both warbling of one song, both in one key,
As if our hands, our sides, voices, and minds
Had been incorporate. So we grew together,
like to a double cherry, seeming parted,
But yet an union in partition,
Two lovely berries molded on one stem;
So, with two seeming bodies but one heart,
Two of the first, like coats in heraldry,
Due but to one and crownèd with one crest.
And will you rend our ancient love asunder,
To join with men in scorning your poor friend?
It is not friendly, 'tis not maidenly.
Our sex, as well as I, may chide you for it,
Though I alone do feel the injury.

Hermia

I am amazèd at your passionate words.
I scorn you not. It seems that you scorn me.

Helena

Have you not set Lysander, as in scorn,
To follow me and praise my eyes and face?
And made your other love, Demetrius,
Who even but now did spurn me with his foot,
To call me goddess, nymph, divine, and rare,
Precious, celestial? Wherefore speaks he this
To her he hates? And wherefore doth Lysander
Deny your love, so rich within his soul,
And tender me, forsooth, affection,
But by your setting on, by your consent?
What though I be not so in grace as you,
So hung upon with love, so fortunate,
But miserable most, to love unloved?

This you should pity rather than despise.

Hermia

I understand not what you mean by this.

Helena

Ay, do! Persever, counterfeit sad looks,
Make mouths upon me when I turn my back,
Wink each at other, hold the sweet jest up.
This sport, well carried, shall be chronicled.
If you have any pity, grace, or manners,
You would not make me such an argument.
But fare ye well. 'Tis partly my own fault,
Which death, or absence, soon shall remedy.

Lysander

Stay, gentle Helena; hear my excuse,
My love, my life, my soul, fair Helena!

Helena

O excellent!

Hermia [to Lysander]   Sweet, do not scorn her so.

Demetrius [to Lysander]

If she cannot entreat, I can compel.

Lysander

Thou canst compel no more than she entreat.
Thy threats have no more strength than her weak prayers.
Helen, I love thee, by my life, I do!
I swear by that which I will lose for thee,
To prove him false that says I love thee not.

Demetrius [to Helena]

I say I love thee more than he can do.

Lysander

If thou say so, withdraw, and prove it too.

Demetrius

Quick, come!

Hermia   Lysander, whereto tends all this?

Lysander

Away, you Ethiope!

                              [*He tries to break away from Hermia.*]

Demetrius   No, no; he'll
    Seem to break loose; take on as you would follow,
    But yet come not. You are a tame man. Go!
Lysander [*to Hermia*]
    Hang off, thou cat, thou burr! Vile thing, let loose,
    Or I will shake thee from me like a serpent!
Hermia
    Why are you grown so rude? What change is this,
    Sweet love?
Lysander   Thy love? Out, tawny Tartar, out!
    Out, loathèd med'cine! O hated potion, hence!
Hermia
    Do you not jest?
Helena   Yes, sooth, and so do you.
Lysander
    Demetrius, I will keep my word with thee.
Demetrius
    I would I had your bond, for I perceive
    A weak bond holds you. I'll not trust your word.
Lysander
    What, should I hurt her, strike her, kill her dead?
    Although I hate her, I'll not harm her so.
Hermia
    What, can you do me greater harm than hate?
    Hate me? Wherefore? O me, what news, my love?
    Am not I Hermia? Are not you Lysander?
    I am as fair now as I was erewhile.
    Since night you loved me; yet since night you left me.
    Why, then you left me—O, the gods forbid!—
    In earnest, shall I say?
Lysander   Ay, by my life!
    And never did desire to see thee more.
    Therefore be out of hope, of question, of doubt;
    Be certain, nothing truer. 'Tis no jest
    That I do hate thee and love Helena.

Hermia [*to Helena*]

 O me! You juggler! You cankerblossom!
 You thief of love! What, have you come by night
 And stol'n my love's heart from him?

Helena   Fine, i' faith!

 Have you no modesty, no maiden shame,
 No touch of bashfulness? What, will you tear
 Impatient answers from my gentle tongue?
 Fie, fie! You counterfeit, you puppet, you!

Hermia

 "Puppet"? Why, so! Ay, that way goes the game.
 Now I perceive that she hath made compare
 Between our statures; she hath urged her height,
 And with her personage, her tall personage,
 Her height, forsooth, she hath prevailed with him.
 And are you grown so high in his esteem
 Because I am so dwarfish and so low?
 How low am I, thou painted maypole? Speak!
 How low am I? I am not yet so low
 But that my nails can reach unto thine eyes.

         [*She flails at Helena but is restrained.*]

Helena

 I pray you, though you mock me, gentlemen,
 Let her not hurt me. I was never curst;
 I have no gift at all in shrewishness;
 I am a right maid for my cowardice.
 Let her not strike me. You perhaps may think,
 Because she is something lower man myself,
 That I can match her.

Hermia   Lower? Hark, again!

Helena

 Good Hermia, do not be so bitter with me.
 I evermore did love you, Hermia,
 Did ever keep your counsels, never wronged you,
 Save that, in love unto Demetrius,

I told him of your stealth unto this wood.
He followed you; for love I followed him.
But he hath chid me hence and threatened me
To strike me, spurn me, nay, to kill me too.
And now, so you will let me quiet go,
To Athens will I bear my folly back
And follow you no further. Let me go.
You see how simple and how fond I am.

Hermia

Why, get you gone. Who is 't that hinders you?

Helena

A foolish heart, that I leave here behind.

Hermia

What, with Lysander?

Helena   With Demetrius.

Lysander

Be not afraid; she shall not harm thee, Helena.

Demetrius

No, sir, she shall not, though you take her part.

Helena

O, when she is angry, she is keen and shrewd.
She was a vixen when she went to school;
And though she be but little, she is fierce.

Hermia

"Little" again? Nothing but "low" and "little"?
Why will you suffer her to flout me thus?
Let me come to her.

Lysander   Get you gone, you dwarf!
You minimus, of hindering knotgrass made!
You bead, you acorn!

Demetrius   You are too officious
In her behalf that scorns your services.
Let her alone. Speak not of Helena;
Take not her part. For, if thou dost intend
Never so little show of love to her,
Thou shalt aby it.

Lysander   Now she holds me not.
    Now follow, if thou dar'st, to try whose right,
    Of thine or mine, is most in Helena.   [*Exit.*]
Demetrius
    Follow? Nay, I'll go with thee, cheek by jowl.
                                    [*Exit, following Lysander.*]
Hermia
    You, mistress, all this coil is 'long of you.
    Nay, go not back.
Helena   I will not trust you, I,
    Nor longer stay in your curst company.
    Your hands than mine are quicker for a fray;
    My legs are longer, though, to run away.   [*Exit.*]
Hermia
    I am amazed and know not what to say.   [*Exit.*]

                    Oberon and Puck come forward.

Oberon
    This is thy negligence. Still thou mistak'st,
    Or else committ'st thy knaveries willfully.
Puck
    Believe me, king of shadows, I mistook.
    Did not you tell me I should know the man
    By the Athenian garments he had on?
    And so far blameless proves my enterprise
    That I have 'nointed an Athenian's eyes;
    And so far am I glad it so did sort,
    As this their jangling I esteem a sport.
Oberon
    Thou seest these lovers seek a place to fight.
    Hie therefore, Robin, overcast the night;
    The starry welkin cover thou anon
    With drooping fog as black as Acheron,
    And lead these testy rivals so astray
    As one come not within another's way.
    Like to Lysander sometimes frame thy tongue,

Then stir Demetrius up with bitter wrong;
And sometimes rail thou like Demetrius.
And from each other look thou lead them thus,
Till o'er their brows death-counterfeiting sleep
With leaden legs and batty wings doth creep.
Then crush this herb into Lysander's eye,

[giving herb]

Whose liquor hath this virtuous property,
To take from thence all error with his might
And make his eyeballs roll with wonted sight.
When they next wake, all this derision
Shall seem a dream and fruitless vision,
And back to Athens shall the lovers wend
With league whose date till death shall never end.
Whiles I in this affair do thee employ,
I'll to my queen and beg her Indian boy;
And then I will her charmèd eye release
From monster's view, and all things shall be peace.

Puck

My fairy lord, this must be done with haste,
For night's swift dragons cut the clouds full fast,
And yonder shines Aurora's harbinger,
At whose approach ghosts, wand'ring here and there,
Troop home to churchyards. Damnèd spirits all,
That in crossways and floods have burial,
Already to their wormy beds are gone.
For fear lest day should look their shames upon,
They willfully themselves exile from light
And must for aye consort with black-browed night.

Oberon

But we are spirits of another sort.
I with the Morning's love have oft made sport,
And, like a forester, the groves may tread
Even till the eastern gate, all fiery red,
Opening on Neptune with fair blessèd beams,

Turns into yellow gold his salt green streams.
But notwithstanding, haste, make no delay.
We may effect this business yet ere day.   [*Exit.*]

Puck

    Up and down, up and down,
    I will lead them up and down.
    I am feared in field and town.
    Goblin, lead them up and down.
Here comes one.

Enter Lysander.

Lysander

Where art thou, proud Demetrius? Speak thou now.

Puck [*mimicking Demetrius*]

Here, villain, drawn and ready. Where art thou?

Lysander

I will be with thee straight.

Puck   Follow me, then,
To plainer ground.

[*Lysander wanders about, following the voice.*]

Enter Demetrius.

Demetrius   Lysander! Speak again!
Thou runaway, thou coward, art thou fled?
Speak! In some bush? Where dost thou hide thy head?

Puck [*mimicking Lysander*]

Thou coward, art thou bragging to the stars,
Telling the bushes that thou look'st for wars,
And wilt not come? Come, recreant; come, thou child,
I'll whip thee with a rod. He is defiled
That draws a sword on thee.

Demetrius   Yea, art thou there?

Puck

Follow my voice. We'll try no manhood here.

[*Exeunt.*]

[Lysander returns.]

Lysander
>He goes before me and still dares me on.
>When I come where he calls, then he is gone.
>The villain is much lighter-heeled than I.
>I followed fast, but faster he did fly,
>That fallen am I in dark uneven way,
>And here will rest me. *[He lies down.]* Come, thou gentle day!
>For if but once thou show me thy gray light,
>I'll find Demetrius and revenge this spite.   *[He sleeps.]*

[Enter] Robin [Puck] and Demetrius.

Puck
>Ho, ho, ho! Coward, why com'st thou not?

Demetrius
>Abide me, if thou dar'st; for well I wot
>Thou runn'st before me, shifting every place,
>And dar'st not stand nor look me in the face.
>Where art thou now?

Puck   Come hither. I am here.

Demetrius
>Nay, then, thou mock'st me. Thou shalt buy this dear,
>If ever I thy face by daylight see.
>Now go thy way. Faintness constraineth me
>To measure out my length, on this cold bed.
>By day's approach look to be visited.

[He lies down and sleeps.]

Enter Helena.

Helena
>O weary night, O long and tedious night,
>   Abate thy hours! Shine comforts from the east,
>That I may back to Athens by daylight
>   From these that my poor company detest;
>And sleep, that sometimes shuts up sorrow's eye,
>Steal me awhile from mine own company.

[She lies down and] sleep[s].

Puck

      Yet but three? Come one more;
      Two of both kinds makes up four.
      Here she comes, curst and sad.
      Cupid is a knavish lad,
      Thus to make poor females mad.

[Enter Hermia.]

Hermia

  Never so weary, never so in woe,
    Bedabbled with the dew and torn with briers,
  I can no further crawl, no further go;
    My legs can keep no pace with my desires.
  Here will I rest me till the break of day.
  Heavens shield Lysander, if they mean a fray!

[She lies down and sleeps.]

Puck

      On the ground
      Sleep sound.
      I'll apply
      To your eye,
    Gentle lover, remedy.

[He squeezes the juice on Lysander's eyes.]

      When thou wak'st,
      Thou tak'st
      True delight
      In the sight
  Of thy former lady's eye;
  And the country proverb known,
  That every man should take his own,
  In your waking shall be shown:
    Jack shall have Jill;
    Naught shall go ill;
  The man shall have his mare again, and all shall be well.

[Exit. The four sleeping lovers remain.]

4.1 ENTER [TITANIA,] QUEEN OF FAIRIES, AND [BOTTOM THE] CLOWN, AND FAIRIES; AND [OBERON,] THE KING, BEHIND THEM.

Titania
> Come, sit thee down upon this flowery bed,
>> While I thy amiable cheeks do coy,
> And stick muskroses in thy sleek smooth head,
>> And kiss thy fair large ears, my gentle joy.

[They recline.]

Bottom   Where's Peaseblossom?

Peaseblossom   Ready.

Bottom   Scratch my head, Peaseblossom. Where's Monsieur Cobweb?

Cobweb   Ready.

Bottom   Monsieur Cobweb, good monsieur, get you your weapons in your hand, and kill me a red-hipped humble-bee on the top of a thistle; and, good monsieur, bring me the honey bag. Do not fret yourself too much in the action, monsieur; and, good monsieur, have a care the honey bag break not. I would be loath to have you overflown with a honey bag, signor. *[Exit Cobweb.]* Where's Monsieur Mustardseed?

Mustardseed   Ready.

Bottom   Give me your neaf, Monsieur Mustardseed. Pray you, leave your courtesy, good monsieur.

Mustardseed   What's your will?

Bottom   Nothing, good monsieur, but to help Cavalery Cobweb to scratch. I must to the barber's, monsieur, for methinks I am marvelous hairy about the face; and I am such a tender ass, if my hair do but tickle me I must scratch.

Titania   What, wilt thou hear some music, my sweet love?

Bottom   I have a reasonable good ear in music. Let's have the tongs and the bones.

[Music: tongs rural music.]

Titania
> Or say, sweet love, what thou desirest to eat.

Bottom   Truly, a peck of provender. I could munch your good dry oats. Methinks I have a great desire to a bottle of hay. Good hay, sweet hay, hath no fellow.

Titania

   I have a venturous fairy that shall seek

   The squirrel's hoard, and fetch thee new nuts.

Bottom   I had rather have a handful or two of dried peas. But, I pray
   you, let none of your people stir me. I have an exposition of sleep
   come upon me.

Titania

   Sleep thou, and I will wind thee in my arms.

Fairies, begone, and be all ways away.

[*Exeunt Fairies.*]

So doth the woodbine the sweet honeysuckle
Gently entwist; the female ivy so
Enrings the barky fingers of the elm.
O, how I love thee! How I dote on thee!

[*They sleep.*]

Enter Robin Goodfellow [Puck].

Oberon [*coming forward*]
    Welcome, good Robin. Seest thou this sweet sight?
    Her dotage now I do begin to pity.
    For, meeting her of late behind the wood
    Seeking sweet favors for this hateful fool,
    I did upbraid her and fall out with her.
    For she his hairy temples then had rounded
    With coronet of fresh and fragrant flowers;
    And that same dew, which sometime on the buds
    Was wont to swell like round and orient pearls,
    Stood now within the pretty flowerets' eyes
    Like tears that did their own disgrace bewail.
    When I had at my pleasure taunted her,
    And she in mild terms begged my patience,
    I then did ask of her her changeling child,
    Which straight she gave me, and her fairy sent
    To bear him to my bower in Fairyland.
    And, now I have the boy, I will undo
    This hateful imperfection of her eyes.
    And, gentle Puck, take this transformèd scalp
    From off the head of this Athenian swain,
    That he, awaking when the other do,
    May all to Athens back again repair,
    And think no more of this night's accidents
    But as me fierce vexation of a dream.
    But first I will release the Fairy Queen.

[*He squeezes an herb on her eyes.*]

    Be as thou wast wont to be;
    See as thou wast wont to see.
    Dian's bud o'er Cupid's flower
    Hath such force and blessèd power.
Now, my Titania, wake you, my sweet queen.

Titania [*awaking*]

    My Oberon! What visions have I seen!
    Methought I was enamored of an ass.

Oberon

    There lies your love.

Titania   How came these things to pass?
    O, how mine eyes do loathe his visage now!

Oberon

    Silence awhile. Robin, take off this head.
    Titania, music call, and strike more dead
    Than common sleep of all these five the sense.

Titania

    Music, ho! Music, such as charmeth sleep!   [*Music.*]

Puck [*removing the ass head*]

    Now, when thou wak'st, with thine own fool's eyes peep.

Oberon

    Sound, music! Come, my queen, take hands with me,
    And rock the ground whereon these sleepers be.

                              [*They dance.*]

    Now thou and I are new in amity,
    And will tomorrow midnight solemnly
    Dance in Duke Theseus' house triumphantly,
    And bless it to all fair prosperity.
    There shall the pairs of faithful lovers be
    Wedded, with Theseus, all in jollity.

Puck

        Fairy King, attend, and mark:
        I do hear the morning lark.

Oberon

        Then, my queen, in silence sad,
        Trip we after night's shade.

> We the globe can compass soon,
> Swifter than the wandering moon.

Titania

> Come, my lord, and in our flight
> Tell me how it came this night
> That I sleeping here was found
> With these mortals on the ground.
>   *Exeunt [Oberon, Titania, and Puck]. Wind horn [within].*

> *Enter Theseus and all his train; [Hippolyta, Egeus].*

Theseus

> Go, one of you, find out the forester,
> For now our observation is performed;
> And since we have the vaward of the day,
> My love shall hear the music of my hounds.
> Uncouple in the western valley; let them go.
> Dispatch, I say, and find the forester.
>
>   *[Exit an Attendant.]*
>
> We will, fair queen, up to the mountain's top
> And mark the musical confusion
> Of hounds and echo in conjunction.

Hippolyta

> I was with Hercules and Cadmus once
> When in a wood of Crete they bayed the bear
> With hounds of Sparta. Never did I hear
> Such gallant chiding; for, besides the groves,
> The skies, the fountains, every region near
> Seemed all one mutual cry. I never heard
> So musical a discord, such sweet thunder.

Theseus

> My hounds are bred out of the Spartan kind,
> So flewed, so sanded; and their heads are hung
> With ears that sweep away the morning dew;
> Crook-kneed, and dewlapped like Thessalian bulls;
> Slow in pursuit, but matched in mouth like bells,
> Each under each. A cry more tunable

Was never holloed to nor cheered with horn
In Crete, in Sparta, nor in Thessaly.
Judge when you hear. [*He sees the sleepers.*] But soft!
    What nymphs are these?

Egeus

My lord, this is my daughter here asleep,
And this Lysander; this Demetrius is;
This Helena, old Nedar's Helena.
I wonder of their being here together.

Theseus

No doubt they rose up early to observe
The rite of May, and hearing our intent,
Came here in grace of our solemnity.
But speak, Egeus. Is not this the day
That Hermia should give answer of her choice?

Egeus   It is, my lord.

Theseus

Go bid the huntsmen wake them with their horns.

[*Exit an Attendant.*]

Shout within. Wind horns. They all start up.

Good morrow, friends. Saint Valentine is past.
Begin these woodbirds but to couple now?

Lysander

Pardon, my lord.   [*They kneel.*]

Theseus   I pray you all, stand up.

[*They stand.*]

I know you two are rival enemies;
How comes this gentle concord in the world,
That hatred is so far from jealousy
To sleep by hate and fear no enmity?

Lysander

My lord, I shall reply amazedly,
Half sleep, half waking; but as yet, I swear,
I cannot truly say how I came here.
But, as I think—for truly would I speak,

And now I do bethink me, so it is—
I came with Hermia hither. Our intent
Was to be gone from Athens, where we might,
Without the peril of the Athenian law—

Egeus

Enough, enough, my lord; you have enough.
I beg the law, the law, upon his head.
They would have stol'n away; they would, Demetrius,
Thereby to have defeated you and me,
You of your wife and me of my consent,
Of my consent that she should be your wife.

Demetrius

My lord, fair Helen told me of their stealth,
Of this their purpose hither to this wood,
And I in fury hither followed them,
Fair Helena in fancy following me.
But, my good lord, I wot not by what power—
But by some power it is—my love to Hermia,
Melted as the snow, seems to me now
As the remembrance of an idle gaud
Which in my childhood I did dote upon;
And all the faith, the virtue of my heart,
The object and the pleasure of mine eye,
Is only Helena. To her, my lord,
Was I betrothed ere I saw Hermia,
But like a sickness did I loathe this food;
But, as in health, come to my natural taste,
Now I do wish it, love it, long for it,
And will forevermore be true to it.

Theseus

Fair lovers, you are fortunately met.
Of this discourse we more will hear anon.
Egeus, I will overbear your will;
For in the temple, by and by, with us
These couples shall eternally be knit.
And, for the morning now is something worn,

Our purposed hunting shall be set aside.
Away with us to Athens. Three and three.
We'll hold a feast in great solemnity.
Come, Hippolyta.

[*Exeunt Theseus, Hippolyta, Egeus, and train.*]

Demetrius
These things seem small and undistinguishable,
Like far-off mountains turnèd into clouds.

Hermia
Methinks I see these things with parted eye,
When everything seems double.

Helena   So methinks;
And I have found Demetrius like a jewel,
Mine own, and not mine own.

Demetrius   Are you sure
That we are awake? It seems to me
That yet we sleep, we dream. Do not you think
The Duke was here, and bid us follow him?

Hermia
Yea, and my father.

Helena   And Hippolyta.

Lysander
And he did bid us follow to the temple.

Demetrius
Why, then, we are awake. Let's follow him,
And by the way let us recount our dreams.

[*Exeunt the lovers.*]

Bottom [*awaking*]   When my cue comes, call me, and I will answer.
My next is "Most fair Pyramus." Heigh-ho! Peter Quince! Flute, the
bellows mender! Snout, the tinker! Starveling! God's my life, stolen
hence and left me asleep! I have had a most rare vision. I have had a
dream, past the wit of man to say what dream it was. Man is but an
ass if he go about to expound this dream. Methought I was—there
is no man can tell what. Methought I was—and methought I had—
but man is but a patched fool if he will offer to say what methought
I had. The eye of man hath not heard, the ear of man hath not

seen, man's hand is not able to taste, his tongue to conceive, nor his heart to report, what my dream was. I will get Peter Quince to write a ballad of this dream. It shall be called "Bottom's Dream," because it hath no bottom; and I will sing it in the latter end of a play, before the Duke. Peradventure, to make it the more gracious, I shall sing it at her death.   [*Exit.*]

4.2 ENTER QUINCE, FLUTE, [SNOUT, AND STARVELING].

Quince   Have you sent to Bottom's house? Is he come home yet?

Starveling   He cannot be heard of. Out of doubt he is transported.

Flute   If he come not, then the play is marred. It goes not forward. Doth it?

Quince   It is not possible. You have not a man in all Athens able to discharge Pyramus but he.

Flute   No, he hath simply the best wit of any handicraft man in Athens.

Quince   Yea, and the best person too, and he is a very paramour for a sweet voice.

Flute   You must say "paragon." A paramour is, God bless us, a thing of naught.

Enter Snug the joiner.

Snug   Masters, the Duke is coming from the temple, and there is two or three lords and ladies more married. If our sport had gone forward, we had all been made men.

Flute   O sweet bully Bottom! Thus hath he lost sixpence a day during his life; he could not have scaped sixpence a day. An the Duke had not given him sixpence a day for playing Pyramus, I'll be hanged. He would have deserved it. Sixpence a day in Pyramus, or nothing.

Enter Bottom.

Bottom   Where are these lads? Where are these hearts?

Quince   Bottom! O most courageous day! O most happy hour!

Bottom   Masters, I am to discourse wonders. But ask me not what; for if I tell you, I am no true Athenian. I will tell you everything, right as it fell out.

Quince   Let us hear, sweet Bottom.

Bottom   Not a word of me. All that I will tell you is that the Duke hath dined. Get your apparel together, good strings to your beards, new ribbons to your pumps; meet presently at the palace; every man look o'er his part; for the short and the long is, our play is preferred. In any case, let Thisbe have clean linen; and let not him that plays the lion pare his nails, for they shall hang out for the lion's claws. And, most dear actors, eat no onions nor garlic, for we are to utter sweet breath; and I do not doubt but to hear them say it is a sweet comedy. No more words. Away! Go, away!

[*Exeunt.*]

5.1 ENTER THESEUS, HIPPOLYTA, AND PHILOSTRATE,
[LORDS, AND ATTENDANTS].

Hippolyta
    'Tis strange, my Theseus, that these lovers speak of.
Theseus
    More strange than true. I never may believe
    These antique fables nor these fairy toys.
    Lovers and madmen have such seething brains,
    Such shaping fantasies, that apprehend
    More than cool reason ever comprehends.
    The lunatic, the lover, and the poet
    Are of imagination all compact.
    One sees more devils than vast hell can hold;
    That is the madman. The lover, all as frantic,
    Sees Helen's beauty in a brow of Egypt.
    The poet's eye, in a fine frenzy rolling,
    Doth glance from heaven to earth, from earth to heaven;
    And as imagination bodies forth
    The forms of things unknown, the poet's pen
    Turns them to shapes and gives to airy nothing
    A local habitation and a name.
    Such tricks hath strong imagination
    That, if it would but apprehend some joy,
    It comprehends some bringer of that joy;
    Or in the night, imagining some fear,
    How easy is a bush supposed a bear!
Hippolyta
    But all the story of the night told over,
    And all their minds transfigured so together,
    More witnesseth than fancy's images
    And grows to something of great constancy;
    But, howsoever, strange and admirable.

        Enter lovers: Lysander, Demetrius, Hermia, and Helena.
Theseus
    Here come the lovers, full of joy and mirth.

Joy, gentle friends! Joy and fresh days of love
Accompany your hearts!

Lysander   More than to us

Wait in your royal walks, your board, your bed!

Theseus

Come now, what masques, what dances shall we have,
To wear away this long age of three hours
Between our after-supper and bedtime?
Where is our usual manager of mirth?
What revels are in hand? Is there no play
To ease the anguish of a torturing hour?
Call Philostrate.

Philostrate   Here, mighty Theseus.

Theseus

Say, what abridgment have you for this evening?
What masque? What music? How shall we beguile
The lazy time, if not with some delight?

Philostrate [*giving him a paper*]

There is a brief how many sports are ripe.
Make choice of which Your Highness will see first.

Theseus [*reads*]

"The battle with the Centaurs, to be sung
By an Athenian eunuch to the harp"?
We'll none of that. That have I told my love,
In glory of my kinsman Hercules.
[*He reads.*] "The riot of the tipsy Bacchanals,
Tearing the Thracian singer in their rage"?
That is an old device; and it was played
When I from Thebes came last a conqueror.
[*He reads.*] "The thrice three Muses mourning for the death
Of Learning, late deceased in beggary"?
That is some satire, keen and critical,
Not sorting with a nuptial ceremony.
[*He reads.*] "A tedious brief scene of young Pyramus
And his love Thisbe; very tragical mirth"?
Merry and tragical? Tedious and brief?

That is, hot ice and wondrous strange snow.
How shall we find the concord of this discord?
Philostrate
   A play there is, my lord, some ten words long,
   Which is as brief as I have known a play;
   But by ten words, my lord, it is too long,
   Which makes it tedious. For in all the play

There is not one word apt, one player fitted.
And tragical, my noble lord, it is,
For Pyramus therein doth kill himself.
Which, when I saw rehearsed, I must confess,
Made mine eyes water; but more merry tears
The passion of loud laughter never shed.

Theseus   What are they that do play it?

Philostrate
Hardhanded men that work in Athens here,
Which never labored in their minds till now,
And now have toiled their unbreathed memories
With this same play, against your nuptial.

Theseus
And we will hear it.

Philostrate   No, my noble lord,
It is not for you. I have heard it over,
And it is nothing, nothing in the world;
Unless you can find sport in their intents,
Extremely stretched and conned with cruel pain
To do you service.

Theseus   I will hear that play;
For never anything can be amiss
When, simpleness and duty tender it.
Go, bring them in; and take your places, ladies.
                    [*Philostrate goes to summon the players.*]

Hippolyta
I love not to see wretchedness o'ercharged,
And duty in his service perishing.

Theseus
Why, gentle sweet, you shall see no such thing.

Hippolyta
He says they can do nothing in this kind.

Theseus
The kinder we, to give them thanks for nothing.
Our sport shall be to take what they mistake;
And what poor duty cannot do, noble respect

Takes it in might, not merit.
Where I have come, great clerks have purposèd
To greet me with premeditated welcomes;
Where I have seen them shiver and look pale,
Make periods in the midst of sentences,
Throttle their practiced accent in their fears,
And in conclusion dumbly have broke off,
Not paying me a welcome. Trust me, sweet,
Out of this silence yet I picked a welcome;
And in the modesty of fearful duty
I read as much as from the rattling tongue
Of saucy and audacious eloquence.
Love, therefore, and tongue-tied simplicity
In least speak most, to my capacity.

[Philostrate returns.]

Philostrate
So please Your Grace, the Prologue is addressed.
Theseus   Let him approach.   *[A flourish of trumpets.]*

Enter the Prologue [Quince].

Prologue
If we offend, it is with our good will.
    That you should think, we come not to offend,
But with good will. To show our simple skill,
    That is the true beginning of our end.
Consider, then, we come but in despite.
    We do not come, as minding to content you,
Our true intent is. All for your delight
    We are not here. That you should here repent you,
The actors are at hand; and, by their show,
You shall know all that you are like to know.
Theseus   This fellow doth not stand upon points.
Lysander   He hath rid his prologue like a rough colt; he knows not the stop. A good moral, my lord: it is not enough to speak, but to speak true.

Hippolyta   Indeed, he hath played on his prologue like a child on a
recorder: a sound, but not in government.

Theseus   His speech was like a tangled chain: nothing impaired, but
all disordered. Who is next?

Enter Pyramus [Bottom], and Thisbe [Flute], and Wall [Snout], and
Moonshine [Starveling], and Lion [Snug].

Prologue
Gentles, perchance you wonder at this show;
    But wonder on, till truth make all things plain.
This man is Pyramus, if you would know;
    This beauteous lady Thisbe is, certain.
This man with lime and roughcast doth present
    Wall, that vile wall which did these lovers sunder;
And through Wall's chink, poor souls, they are content
    To whisper. At the which let no man wonder.
This man, with lantern, dog, and bush of thorn,
    Presenteth Moonshine; for, if you will know,
By moonshine did these lovers think no scorn
    To meet at Ninus' tomb, there, there to woo.
This grisly beast, which Lion hight by name,
    The trusty Thisbe coming first by night
Did scare away, or rather did affright;
    And as she fled, her mantle she did fall,
    Which Lion vile with bloody mouth did stain.
Anon comes Pyramus, sweet youth and tall,
    And finds his trusty Thisbe's mantle slain;
Whereat, with blade, with bloody, blameful blade,
    He bravely broached his boiling bloody breast.
And Thisbe, tarrying in mulberry shade,
    His dagger drew, and died. For all the rest,
Let Lion, Moonshine, Wall, and lovers twain
At large discourse, while here they do remain.

                [Exeunt Lion, Thisbe, and Moonshine.]

Theseus   I wonder if the lion be to speak.

Demetrius   No wonder, my lord. One lion may, when many asses do.

Wall

> In this same interlude it doth befall
> That I, one Snout by name, present a wall;
> And such a wall as I would have you think
> That had in it a crannied hole or chink,
> Through which the lovers, Pyramus and Thisbe,
> Did whisper often, very secretly.
> This loam, this roughcast, and this stone doth show
> That I am that same wall; the truth is so.
> And this the cranny is, right and sinister,
> Through which the fearful lovers are to whisper.

Theseus   Would you desire lime and hair to speak better?

Demetrius   It is the wittiest partition that ever I heard discourse, my
lord.

[Pyramus comes forward.]

Theseus   Pyramus draws near the wall. Silence!

Pyramus

> O grim-looked night! O night with hue so black!
>> O night, which ever art when day is not!
> O night, O night! Alack, alack, alack,
>> I fear my Thisbe's promise is forgot.
> And thou, O wall, O sweet, O lovely wall,
>> That stand'st between her father's ground and mine,
> Thou wall, O wall, O sweet and lovely wall,
>> Show me thy chink, to blink through with mine eyne.

[Wall makes a chink with his fingers.]

> Thanks, courteous wall. Jove shield thee well for this.
>> But what see I? No Thisbe do I see.
> O wicked wall, through whom I see no bliss!
>> Cursed be thy stones for thus deceiving me!

Theseus   The wall, methinks, being sensible, should curse again.

Pyramus   No, in truth, sir, he should not. "Deceiving me" is Thisbe's
cue: she is to enter now, and I am to spy her through the wall. You
shall see, it will fall pat as I told you. Yonder she comes.

Enter Thisbe.

Thisbe

O wall, full often hast thou heard my moans
  For parting my fair Pyramus and me.
My cherry lips have often kissed thy stones,
  Thy stones with lime and hair knit up in thee.

Pyramus

I see a voice. Now will I to the chink,
  To spy an I can hear my Thisbe's face.
Thisbe!

Thisbe   My love! Thou art my love, I think.

Pyramus

  Think what thou wilt, I am thy lover's grace,
And like Limander am I trusty still.

Thisbe

And I like Helen, till the Fates me kill.

Pyramus

Not Shafalus to Procrus was so true.

Thisbe

As Shafalus to Procrus, I to you.

Pyramus

O, kiss me through the hole of this vile wall!

Thisbe

I kiss the wall's hole, not your lips at all.

Pyramus

Wilt thou at Ninny's tomb meet me straightway?

Thisbe

'Tide life, 'tide death, I come without delay.

                              [*Exeunt Pyramus and Thisbe.*]

Wall

Thus have I, Wall, my part dischargèd so;
And, being done, thus Wall away doth go.   [*Exit.*]

Theseus   Now is the mural down between the two neighbors.

Demetrius   No remedy, my lord, when walls are so willful to hear
  without warning.

Hippolyta   This is the silliest stuff that ever I heard.

Theseus   The best in this kind are but shadows; and the worst are no worse, if imagination amend them.

Hippolyta   It must be your imagination then, and not theirs.

Theseus   If we imagine no worse of them than they of themselves, they may pass for excellent men. Here come two noble beasts in, a man and a lion.

Enter Lion and Moonshine.

Lion

You, ladies, you, whose gentle hearts do fear
    The smallest monstrous mouse that creeps on floor,
May now perchance both quake and tremble here,
    When lion rough in wildest rage doth roar.
Then know that I, as Snug the joiner, am
A lion fell, nor else no lion's dam;
For, if I should as lion come in strife
Into this place, 'twere pity on my life.

Theseus   A very gentle beast, and of a good conscience.

Demetrius   The very best at a beast, my lord, that e'er I saw.

Lysander   This lion is a very fox for his valor.

Theseus   True; and a goose for his discretion.

Demetrius   Not so, my lord, for his valor cannot carry his discretion, and the fox carries the goose.

Theseus   His discretion, I am sure, cannot carry his valor; for the goose carries not the fox. It is well. Leave it to his discretion, and let us listen to the moon.

Moon   This lanthorn doth the hornèd moon present—

Demetrius   He should have worn the horns on his head.

Theseus   He is no crescent, and his horns are invisible within the circumference.

Moon

This lanthorn doth the hornèd moon present;
Myself the man i' the moon do seem to be.

Theseus   This is the greatest error of all the rest. The man should be put into the lanthorn. How is it else the man i' the moon?

Demetrius   He dares not come there for the candle, for you see it is already in snuff.

Hippolyta   I am aweary of this moon. Would he would change!

Theseus   It appears, by his small light of discretion, that he is in the wane; but yet, in courtesy, in all reason, we must stay the time.

Lysander   Proceed, Moon.

Moon   All that I have to say is to tell you that the lanthorn is the moon, I, the man i' the moon, this thornbush my thornbush, and this dog my dog.

Demetrius   Why, all these should be in the lanthorn, for all these are in the moon. But silence! Here comes Thisbe.

Enter Thisbe.

Thisbe

This is old Ninny's tomb. Where is my love?

Lion [*roaring*]   O!

Demetrius   Well roared, Lion.

[*Thisbe runs off, dropping her mantle.*]

Theseus   Well run, Thisbe.

Hippolyta   Well shone, Moon. Truly, the moon shines with a good grace.

[*The Lion worries Thisbe's mantle.*]

Theseus   Well moused, Lion.

[*Enter Pyramus; exit Lion.*]

Demetrius   And then came Pyramus.

Lysander   And so the lion vanished.

Pyramus

Sweet Moon, I thank thee for thy sunny beams;
    I thank thee, Moon, for shining now so bright;
For, by thy gracious, golden, glittering gleams,
    I trust to take of truest Thisbe sight.
        But stay, O spite!
        But mark, poor knight,
    What dreadful dole is here?
        Eyes, do you see?

> How can it be?
> O dainty duck! O dear!
>> Thy mantle good,
>> What, stained with blood?
> Approach, ye Furies fell!
>> O Fates, come, come,
>> Cut thread and thrum;
> Quail, crush, conclude, and quell!

Theseus   This passion, and the death of a dear friend, would go near to make a man look sad.

Hippolyta   Beshrew my heart, but I pity the man.

Pyramus

> O, wherefore, Nature, didst thou lions frame?
> Since lion vile hath here deflowered my dear,
> Which is—no, no, which was—the fairest dame
> That lived, that loved, that liked, that looked with cheer.
>> Come, tears, confound,
>> Out, sword, and wound
> The pap of Pyramus;
>> Ay, that left pap,
>> Where heart doth hop.   [*He stabs himself.*]
> Thus die I, thus, thus, thus.
>> Now am I dead,
>> Now am I fled;
> My soul is in the sky.
>> Tongue, lose thy light;
>> Moon, take thy flight.   [*Exit Moonshine.*]
>> Now die, die, die, die, die.   [*Pyramus dies.*]

Demetrius   No die, but an ace, for him; for he is but one.

Lysander   Less than an ace, man; for he is dead, he is nothing.

Theseus   With the help of a surgeon he might yet recover, and yet prove an ass.

Hippolyta   How chance Moonshine is gone before Thisbe comes back and finds her lover?

Theseus   She will find him by starlight.

[*Enter Thisbe.*]

Here she comes; and her passion ends the play.

Hippolyta   Methinks she should not use a long one for such a
Pyramus. I hope she will be brief.

Demetrius   A mote will turn the balance, which Pyramus, which
Thisbe, is the better: he for a man, God warrant us; she for a
woman, God bless us.

Lysander   She hath spied him already with those sweet eyes.

Demetrius   And thus she means, videlicet:

Thisbe

      Asleep, my love?
      What, dead, my dove?
O Pyramus, arise!
      Speak, speak. Quite dumb?
      Dead, dead? A tomb
Must cover thy sweet eyes.
      These lily lips,
      This cherry nose,
These yellow cowslip cheeks,
      Are gone, are gone!
      Lovers, make moan.
His eyes were green as leeks.
      O Sisters Three,
      Come, come to me,
With hands as pale as milk;
      Lay them in gore,
      Since you have shore
With shears his thread of silk.
      Tongue, not a word.
      Come, trusty sword,
Come, blade, my breast imbrue!

                    [*She stabs herself.*]

      And farewell, friends.
      Thus Thisbe ends.
Adieu, adieu, adieu.   [*She dies.*]

Theseus   Moonshine and Lion are left to bury the dead.

Demetrius   Ay, and Wall too.

Bottom [*starting up, as Flute does also*]   No, I assure you, the wall is
down that parted their fathers. Will it please you to see the epilogue,
or to hear a Bergomask dance between two of our company?

[*The other players enter.*]

Theseus   No epilogue, I pray you; for your play needs no excuse.
Never excuse; for when the players are all dead, there need none to
be blamed. Marry, if he that writ it had played Pyramus and hanged
himself in Thisbe's garter, it would have been a fine tragedy; and so
it is, truly, and very notably discharged. But, come, your Bergomask.
Let your epilogue alone.   [*A dance.*]

The iron tongue of midnight hath told twelve.
Lovers, to bed, 'tis almost fairy time.
I fear we shall outsleep the coming morn
As much as we this night have overwatched.
This palpable-gross play hath well beguiled
The heavy gait of night. Sweet friends, to bed.
A fortnight hold we this solemnity,
In nightly revels and new jollity.   [*Exeunt.*]

Enter Puck [*carrying a broom*].

Puck

　　　Now the hungry lion roars,
　　　　And the wolf behowls the moon,
　　　Whilst the heavy plowman snores,
　　　　All with weary task fordone.
　　　Now the wasted brands do glow,
　　　　Whilst the screech owl, screeching loud,
　　　Puts the wretch that lies in woe
　　　　In remembrance of a shroud.
　　　Now it is the time of night
　　　　That the graves, all gaping wide,
　　　Every one lets forth his sprite,
　　　　In the church-way paths to glide.

And we fairies, that do run
   By the triple Hecate's team.
From the presence of the sun,
   Following darkness like a dream,
Now are frolic. Not a mouse
   Shall disturb this hallowed house.
I am sent with broom before,
To sweep the dust behind the door.

Enter [Oberon and Titania,] King and Queen of Fairies,
with all their train.

Oberon

Through the house give glimmering light,
   By the dead and drowsy fire;
Every elf and fairy sprite
   Hop as light as bird from brier;
And this ditty, after me,
Sing, and dance it trippingly.

Titania

First, rehearse your song by rote,
To each word a warbling note.
Hand in hand, with fairy grace,
Will we sing, and bless this place.

[Song and dance.]

Oberon

Now, until the break of day,
Through this house each fairy stray.
To the best bride-bed will we,
Which by us shall blessèd be;
And the issue there create
Ever shall be fortunate.
So shall all the couples three
Ever true in loving be;
And the blots of Nature's hand
Shall not in their issue stand;
Never mole, harelip, nor scar,

Nor mark prodigious, such as are
Despisèd in nativity,
Shall upon their children be.
With this field dew consecrate,
Every fairy take his gait,
And each several chamber bless,
Through this palace, with sweet peace;
And the owner of it blest
Ever shall in safety rest.
Trip away make no stay;
Meet me all by break of day.

Exeunt [Oberon, Titania, and train].

Puck [to the audience]

If we shadows have offended,
Think but this, and all is mended,
That you have but slumbered here
While these visions did appear.
And this weak and idle theme,
No more yielding but a dream,
Gentles, do not reprehend.
If you pardon, we will mend.
And, as I am an honest Puck,
If we have unearnèd luck
Now to scape the serpent's tongue,
We will make amends ere long;
Else the Puck a liar call.
So, good night unto you all.
Give me your hands, if we be friends,
And Robin shall restore amends.   *[Exit.]*

The Taming of the Shrew

The Taming of the Shrew

DRAMATIS PERSONAE

Persons in the Induction: *Christopher Sly*, a tinker and
  beggar, *Hostess* of an alehouse, *a Lord, a Page,
  Servants, Huntsmen, Players*
Baptista, a rich gentleman of Padua
Katharina, the shrew, also called Katharine and Kate,
  Baptista's elder daughter
Bianca, Baptista's younger daughter
Petruchio, a gentleman of Verona, suitor to Katharina
Grumio, Petruchio's servant
Curtis, Nathaniel, Philip, Joseph, Nicholas, Peter, and other
  servants of Petruchio
Gremio, elderly suitor to Bianca
Hortensio, suitor to Bianca
Lucentio, son of Vincentio, in love with Bianca
Tranio, Lucentio's servant
Biondello, Lucentio's servant
Vincentio, a gentleman of Pisa
A *Pedant* (or Merchant) of Mantua
A *Widow*, courted by Hortensio
A *Tailor*
A *Haberdasher*
An *Officer*
Other Servants of Baptista and Lucentio

Scene: Padua, and Petruchio's country house in Italy;
the Induction is located in the countryside and at a
Lord's house in England

INDUCTION.1

Enter Beggar (Christopher Sly) and Hostess.

Sly I'll feeze you, in faith.

Hostess A pair of stocks, you rogue!

Sly You're a baggage. The Slys are no rogues. Look in the chronicles; we came in with Richard Conqueror. Therefore *paucas pallabris*, let the world slide. Sessa!

Hostess You will not pay for the glasses you have burst?

Sly No, not a denier. Go by, Saint Jeronimy, go to thy cold bed and warm thee.

Hostess I know my remedy; I must go fetch the third-borough. [*Exit.*]

Sly Third, or fourth, or fifth borough, I'll answer him by law. I'll not budge an inch, boy. Let him come, and kindly.   *Falls asleep.*

Wind horns [within].
Enter a Lord from hunting, with his train.

Lord
　　Huntsman, I charge thee, tender well my hounds.
　　Breathe Merriman—the poor cur is embossed—
　　And couple Clowder with the deep-mouthed brach.
　　Sawst thou not, boy, how Silver made it good
　　At the hedge corner, in the coldest fault?
　　I would not lose the dog for twenty pound.

First Huntsman
　　Why, Bellman is as good as he, my lord.
　　He cried upon it at the merest loss,
　　And twice today picked out the dullest scent.
　　Trust me, I take him for the better dog.

Lord
　　Thou art a fool. If Echo were as fleet,
　　I would esteem him worth a dozen such.
　　But sup them well and look unto them all.
　　Tomorrow I intend to hunt again.

First Huntsman
　　I will, my lord.

Lord [*seeing Sly*]

What's here? One dead, or drunk? See, doth he breathe?

Second Huntsman [*examining Sly*]

He breathes, my lord. Were he not warmed with ale,
This were a bed but cold to sleep so soundly.

Lord

O monstrous beast, how like a swine he lies!
Grim death, how foul and loathsome is thine image!
Sirs, I will practice on this drunken man.
What think you, if he were conveyed to bed,
Wrapped in sweet clothes, rings put upon his fingers,
A most delicious banquet by his bed,
And brave attendants near him when he wakes,
Would not the beggar then forget himself?

First Huntsman

Believe me, lord, I think he cannot choose.

Second Huntsman

It would seem strange unto him when he waked.

Lord

Even as a flattering dream or worthless fancy.
Then take him up, and manage well the jest.
Carry him gently to my fairest chamber,
And hang it round with all my wanton pictures.
Balm his foul head in warm distillèd waters,
And burn sweet wood to make the lodging sweet.
Procure me music ready when he wakes,
To make a dulcet and a heavenly sound.
And if he chance to speak, be ready straight,
And with a low submissive reverence
Say, "What is it your honor will command?"
Let one attend him with a silver basin
Full of rosewater and bestrewed with flowers;
Another bear the ewer, the third a diaper,
And say, "Will 't please your lordship cool your hands?"
Someone be ready with a costly suit,

And ask him what apparel he will wear;
Another tell him of his hounds and horse,
And that his lady mourns at his disease.
Persuade him that he hath been lunatic,
And when he says he is, say that he dreams,
For he is nothing but a mighty lord.
This do, and do it kindly, gentle sirs.
It will be pastime passing excellent,
If it be husbanded with modesty.

First Huntsman

My lord, I warrant you we will play our part
As he shall think by our true diligence
He is no less than what we say he is.

Lord

Take him up gently, and to bed with him,
And each one to his office when he wakes.

[Some bear out Sly.] Sound trumpets [within].

Sirrah, go see what trumpet 'tis that sounds.

[*Exit a Servingman.*]

Belike some noble gentleman that means,
Traveling some journey, to repose him here.

Enter [a] Servingman.

How now? Who is it?

Servingman   An 't please your honor, players
That offer service to your lordship.

Enter Players.

Lord
Bid them come near.—Now, fellows, you are welcome.

Players   We thank your honor.

Lord
Do you intend to stay with me tonight?

First Player
So please your lordship to accept our duty.

Lord
With all my heart. This fellow I remember
Since once he played a farmer's eldest son.—
'Twas where you wooed the gentlewoman so well.
I have forgot your name, but sure that part
Was aptly fitted and naturally performed.

Second Player
I think 'twas Soto that your honor means.

Lord
'Tis very true. Thou didst it excellent.
Well, you are come to me in happy time,
The rather for I have some sport in hand
Wherein your cunning can assist me much.
There is a lord will hear you play tonight.
But I am doubtful of your modesties,
Lest, overeyeing of his odd behavior—
For yet his honor never heard a play—
You break into some merry passion

And so offend him; for I tell you, sirs,
If you should smile, he grows impatient.

First Player

Fear not, my lord, we can contain ourselves
Were he the veriest antic in the world.

Lord [*to a Servingman*]

Go, sirrah, take them to the buttery,
And give them friendly welcome every one.
Let them want nothing that my house affords.

[*Exit one with the Players.*]

Sirrah, go you to Barthol'mew my page,
And see him dressed in all suits like a lady.
That done, conduct him to the drunkard's chamber,
And call him "madam," do him obeisance.
Tell him from me, as he will win my love,
He bear himself with honorable action
Such as he hath observed in noble ladies
Unto their lords by them accomplishèd.
Such duty to the drunkard let him do
With soft low tongue and lowly courtesy,
And say, "What is 't your honor will command,
Wherein your lady and your humble wife
May show her duty and make known her love?"
And then with kind embracements, tempting kisses,
And with declining head into his bosom,
Bid him shed tears, as being overjoyed
To see her noble lord restored to health,
Who for this seven years hath esteemèd him
No better than a poor and loathsome beggar.
And if the boy have not a woman's gift
To rain a shower of commanded tears,
An onion will do well for such a shift,
Which in a napkin being close conveyed
Shall in despite enforce a watery eye.
See this dispatched with all the haste thou canst.
Anon I'll give thee more instructions.

[*Exit a Servingman.*]

I know the boy will well usurp the grace,
Voice, gait, and action of a gentlewoman.
I long to hear him call the drunkard husband,
And how my men will stay themselves from laughter
When they do homage to this simple peasant.
I'll in to counsel them. Haply my presence
May well abate the overmerry spleen
Which otherwise would grow into extremes.

[*Exeunt.*]

INDUCTION.2

Enter aloft the drunkard [Sly], with attendants; some with apparel,
basin, and ewer and other appurtenances; and Lord.

Sly   For God's sake, a pot of small ale.
First Servingman
    Will 't please your lordship drink a cup of sack?
Second Servingman
    Will 't please your honor taste of these conserves?
Third Servingman
    What raiment will your honor wear today?
Sly   I am Christophero Sly. Call not me "honor" nor "lordship." I
    ne'er drank sack in my life; and if you give me any conserves, give
    me conserves of beef. Ne'er ask me what raiment I'll wear, for I
    have no more doublets than backs, no more stockings than legs,
    nor no more shoes than feet—nay, sometimes more feet than shoes,
    or such shoes as my toes look through the overleather.
Lord
    Heaven cease this idle humor in your honor!
    O, that a mighty man of such descent,
    Of such possessions and so high esteem,
    Should be infusèd with so foul a spirit!
Sly   What, would you make me mad? Am not I Christopher Sly, old
    Sly's son of Burton-heath, by birth a peddler, by education a card-
    maker, by transmutation a bearherd, and now by present profession

a tinker? Ask Marian Hacket, the fat alewife of Wincot, if she know
me not. If she say I am not fourteen pence on the score for sheer
ale, score me up for the lyingest knave in Christendom. What, I am
not bestraught: here's—

Third Servingman

O, this it is that makes your lady mourn!

Second Servingman

O, this is it that makes your servants droop!

Lord

Hence comes it that your kindred shuns your house,
As beaten hence by your strange lunacy.
O noble lord, bethink thee of thy birth.

Call home thy ancient thoughts from banishment,
And banish hence these abject lowly dreams.
Look how thy servants do attend on thee,
Each in his office ready at thy beck.
Wilt thou have music? Hark, Apollo plays,   *Music.*
And twenty cagèd nightingales do sing.
Or wilt thou sleep? We'll have thee to a couch,
Softer and sweeter than the lustful bed
On purpose trimmed up for Semiramis.
Say thou wilt walk; we will bestrew the ground.
Or wilt thou ride? Thy horses shall be trapped,
Their harness studded all with gold and pearl.
Dost thou love hawking? Thou hast hawks will soar
Above the morning lark. Or wilt thou hunt?
Thy hounds shall make the welkin answer them
And fetch shrill echoes from the hollow earth.

First Servingman
Say thou wilt course, thy greyhounds are as swift
As breathèd stags, ay, fleeter than the roe.

Second Servingman
Dost thou love pictures? We will fetch thee straight
Adonis painted by a running brook,
And Cytherea all in sedges hid,
Which seem to move and wanton with her breath,
Even as the waving sedges play wi' th' wind.

Lord
We'll show thee Io as she was a maid,
And how she was beguilèd and surprised,
As lively painted as the deed was done.

Third Servingman
Or Daphne roaming through a thorny wood,
Scratching her legs that one shall swear she bleeds,
And at that sight shall sad Apollo weep,
So workmanly the blood and tears are drawn.

Lord
Thou art a lord, and nothing but a lord.

Thou hast a lady far more beautiful
Than any woman in this waning age.

First Servingman

And till the tears that she hath shed for thee
Like envious floods o`errun her lovely face,
She was the fairest creature in the world;
And yet she is inferior to none.

Sly

Am I a lord? And have I such a lady?
Or do I dream? Or have I dreamed till now?
I do not sleep: I see, I hear, I speak,
I smell sweet savors, and I feel soft things.
Upon my life, I am a lord indeed,
And not a tinker nor Christopher Sly.
Well, bring our lady hither to our sight,
And once again a pot o' the smallest ale.

Second Servingman

Will 't please your mightiness to wash your hands?
O, how we joy to see your wit restored!
O, that once more you knew but what you are!
These fifteen years you have been in a dream,
Or when you waked, so waked as if you slept.

Sly

These fifteen years! By my fay, a goodly nap.
But did I never speak of all that time?

First Servingman

O, yes, my lord, but very idle words;
For though you lay here in this goodly chamber,
Yet would you say ye were beaten out of door,
And rail upon the hostess of the house,
And say you would present her at the leet
Because she brought stone jugs and no sealed quarts.
Sometimes you would call out for Cicely Hacket.

Sly

Ay, the woman's maid of the house.

Third Servingman
    Why, sir, you know no house, nor no such maid,
    Nor no such men as you have reckoned up,
    As Stephen Sly, and old John Naps of Greet,
    And Peter Turf, and Henry Pimpernel,
    And twenty more such names and men as these,
    Which never were, nor no man ever saw.

Sly
    Now Lord be thankèd for my good amends!

All
    Amen.

           Enter [the Page as a] lady, with Attendants.

Sly   I thank thee. Thou shalt not lose by it.

Page
    How fares my noble lord?

Sly   Marry, I fare well,
    For here is cheer enough. Where is my wife?

Page
    Here, noble lord. What is thy will with her?

Sly
    Are you my wife, and will not call me husband?
    My men should call me "lord"; I am your goodman.

Page
    My husband and my lord, my lord and husband,
    I am your wife in all obedience.

Sly
    I know it well.—What must I call her?

Lord   Madam.

Sly   Al'ce madam, or Joan madam?

Lord
    Madam, and nothing else. So lords call ladies.

Sly
    Madam wife, they say that I have dreamed
    And slept above some fifteen year or more.

Page

    Ay, and the time seems thirty unto me,

    Being all this time abandoned from your bed.

Sly

    'Tis much. Servants, leave me and her alone.

    Madam, undress you and come now to bed.

Page

    Thrice-noble lord, let me entreat of you

    To pardon me yet for a night or two,

    Or, if not so, until the sun be set.

    For your physicians have expressly charged,

    In peril to incur your former malady,

    That I should yet absent me from your bed.

    I hope this reason stands for my excuse.

Sly   Ay, it stands so that I may hardly tarry so long. But I would be loath to fall into my dreams again. I will therefore tarry in despite of the flesh and the blood.

Enter a [Servingman as] messenger.

Servingman

    Your honor's players, hearing your amendment,

    Are come to play a pleasant comedy,

    For so your doctors hold it very meet,

    Seeing too much sadness hath congealed your blood,

    And melancholy is the nurse of frenzy.

    Therefore they thought it good you hear a play

    And frame your mind to mirth and merriment,

    Which bars a thousand harms and lengthens life.

Sly   Marry, I will let them play it. Is not a comonty a Christmas gambold or a tumbling-trick?

Page

    No, my good lord, it is more pleasing stuff.

Sly   What, household stuff?

Page   It is a kind of history.

Sly   Well, we'll see 't. Come, madam wife, sit by my side and let the world slip; we shall ne'er be younger.

                  [They sit over the stage.] Flourish.

1.1 ENTER LUCENTIO AND HIS MAN, TRANIO.

Lucentio

> Tranio, since for the great desire I had
> To see fair Padua, nursery of arts,
> I am arrived fore fruitful Lombardy,
> The pleasant garden of great Italy,
> And by my father's love and leave am armed
> With his good will and thy good company,
> My trusty servant, well approved in all,
> Here let us breathe and haply institute
> A course of learning and ingenious studies.
> Pisa, renownèd for grave citizens,
> Gave me my being, and my father first—
> A merchant of great traffic through the world,
> Vincentio, come of the Bentivolii.
> Vincentio's son, brought up in Florence,
> It shall become to serve all hopes conceived
> To deck his fortune with his virtuous deeds.
> And therefore, Tranio, for the time I study,
> Virtue and that part of philosophy
> Will I apply that treats of happiness
> By virtue specially to be achieved.
> Tell me thy mind, for I have Pisa left
> And am to Padua come as he that leaves
> A shallow plash to plunge him in the deep,
> And with satiety seeks to quench his thirst.

Tranio

> Mi *perdonate*, gentle master mine.
> I am in all affected as yourself,
> Glad that you thus continue your resolve
> To suck the sweets of sweet philosophy.
> Only, good master, while we do admire
> This virtue and this moral discipline,
> Let's be no stoics nor no stocks, I pray,
> Or so devote to Aristotle's checks
> As Ovid be an outcast quite abjured.

Balk logic with acquaintance that you have,
And practice rhetoric in your common talk;
Music and poesy use to quicken you;
The mathematics and the metaphysics,
Fall to them as you find your stomach serves you.
No profit grows where is no pleasure ta'en.
In brief, sir, study what you most affect.

Lucentio

Gramercies, Tranio, well dost thou advise.
If, Biondello, thou wert come ashore,
We could at once put us in readiness
And take a lodging fit to entertain
Such friends as time in Padua shall beget.
But stay awhile, what company is this?

Tranio

Master, some show to welcome us to town.

Enter Baptista with his two daughters, Katharina and Bianca;
Gremio, a pantaloon; [and] Hortensio, suitor to Bianca.
Lucentio [and] Tranio stand by.

Baptista
Gentlemen, importune me no farther,
For how I firmly am resolved you know:
That is, not to bestow my youngest daughter
Before I have a husband for the elder.
If either of you both love Katharina,
Because I know you well and love you well,
Leave shall you have to court her at your pleasure.

Gremio
To cart her rather. She's too rough for me.
There, there, Hortensio, will you any wife?

Katharina [to Baptista]
I pray you, sir, is it your will
To make a stale of me amongst these mates?

Hortensio
"Mates," maid? How mean you that? No mates for you,
Unless you were of gentler, milder mold.

Katharina
I' faith, sir, you shall never need to fear;
Iwis it is not halfway to her heart.
But if it were, doubt not her care should be
To comb your noddle with a three-legged stool,
And paint your face, and use you like a fool.

Hortensio
From all such devils, good Lord deliver us!

Gremio   And me too, good Lord!

Tranio [aside to Lucentio]
Husht, master, here's some good pastime toward.
That wench is stark mad or wonderful froward.

Lucentio [aside to Tranio]
But in other's silence do I see
Maid's mild behavior and sobriety.
Peace, Tranio!

Tranio [*aside to Lucentio*]
    Well said, master. Mum, and gaze your fill.
Baptista
    Gentlemen, that I may soon make good
    What I have said—Bianca, get you in.
    And let it not displease thee, good Bianca,
    For I will love thee ne'er the less, my girl.
Katharina   A pretty peat! It is best
    Put finger in the eye, an she knew why.
Bianca
    Sister, content you in my discontent.—
    Sir, to your pleasure humbly I subscribe.
    My books and instruments shall be my company,
    On them to look and practice by myself.
Lucentio [*aside to Tranio*]
    Hark, Tranio, thou mayst hear Minerva speak.
Hortensio
    Signor Baptista, will you be so strange?
    Sorry am I that our good will effects
    Bianca's grief.
Gremio   Why will you mew her up,
    Signor Baptista, for this fiend of hell,
    And make her bear the penance of her tongue?
Baptista
    Gentlemen, content ye. I am resolved.
    Go in, Bianca.   [*Exit Bianca.*]
    And for I know she taketh most delight
    In music, instruments, and poetry,
    Schoolmasters will I keep within my house
    Fit to instruct her youth. If you, Hortensio,
    Or, Signor Gremio, you know any such,
    Prefer them hither; for to cunning men
    I will be very kind, and liberal
    To mine own children in good bringing up.
    And so farewell. Katharina, you may stay,
    For I have more to commune with Bianca.   [*Exit.*]

Katharina

>Why, and I trust I may go too, may I not?
>What, shall I be appointed hours,
>As though, belike, I knew not what to take,
>And what to leave? Ha!   [*Exit.*]

Gremio   You may go to the devil's dam. Your gifts are so good, here's none will hold you.—Their love is not so great, Hortensio, but we may blow our nails together and fast it fairly out. Our cake's dough on both sides. Farewell Yet, for the love I bear my sweet Bianca, if I can by any means light on a fit man to teach her that wherein she delights, I will wish him to her father.

Hortensio   So will I, Signor Gremio. But a word, I pray. Though the nature of our quarrel yet never brooked parle, know now, upon advice, it toucheth us both, that we may yet again have access to our fair mistress and be happy rivals in Bianca's love, to labor and effect one thing specially.

Gremio   What's that, I pray?

Hortensio   Marry, sir, to get a husband for her sister.

Gremio   A husband? A devil.

Hortensio   I say a husband.

Gremio   I say a devil. Think'st thou, Hortensio, though her father be very rich, any man is so very a fool to be married to hell?

Hortensio   Tush, Gremio, though it pass your patience and mine to endure her loud alarums, why, man, there be good fellows in the world, an a man could light on them, would take her with all faults, and money enough.

Gremio   I cannot tell. But I had as lief take her dowry with this condition: to be whipped at the high cross every morning.

Hortensio   Faith, as you say, there's small choice in rotten apples. But come, since this bar in law makes us friends, it shall be so far forth friendly maintained till by helping Baptista's eldest daughter to a husband we set his youngest free for a husband, and then have to 't afresh. Sweet Bianca! Happy man be his dole! He that runs fastest gets the ring. How say you, Signor Gremio?

Gremio   I am agreed, and would I had given him the best horse in Padua to begin his wooing that would thoroughly woo her, wed

her, and bed her and rid the house of her! Come on.   *Exeunt ambo.*
Manent Tranio and Lucentio.

Tranio

I pray, sir, tell me, is it possible
That love should of a sudden take such hold?

Lucentio

O Tranio, till I found it to be true,
I never thought it possible or likely.
But see, while idly I stood looking on,
I found the effect of love in idleness,
And now in plainness do confess to thee,
That art to me as secret and as dear
As Anna to the Queen of Carthage was,
Tranio, I burn, I pine, I perish, Tranio,
If I achieve not this young modest girl.
Counsel me, Tranio, for I know thou canst;
Assist me, Tranio, for I know thou wilt.

Tranio

Master, it is no time to chide you now.
Affection is not rated from the heart.
If love have touched you, naught remains but so,
"Redime te captum quam queas minimo."

Lucentio

Gramercies, lad. Go forward. This contents;
The rest will comfort, for thy counsel's sound.

Tranio

Master, you looked so longly on the maid,
Perhaps you marked not what's the pith of all.

Lucentio

O, yes, I saw sweet beauty in her face,
Such as the daughter of Agenor had,
That made great Jove to humble him to her hand,
When with his knees he kissed the Cretan strand.

Tranio

Saw you no more? Marked you not how her sister

Began to scold and raise up such a storm
That mortal ears might hardly endure the din?

Lucentio

Tranio, I saw her coral lips to move,
And with her breath she did perfume the air.
Sacred and sweet was all I saw in her.

Tranio [*aside*]

Nay, then, 'tis time to stir him from his trance.—
I pray, awake, sir. If you love the maid,
Bend thoughts and wits to achieve her. Thus it stands:
Her elder sister is so curst and shrewd
That till the father rid his hands of her,
Master, your love must live a maid at home,
And therefore has he closely mewed her up,
Because she will not be annoyed with suitors.

Lucentio

Ah, Tranio, what a cruel father's he!
But art thou not advised he took some care
To get her cunning schoolmasters to instruct her?

Tranio

Ay, marry, am I, sir; and now 'tis plotted.

Lucentio

I have it, Tranio.

Tranio   Master, for my hand,
Both our inventions meet and jump in one.

Lucentio

Tell me thine first.

Tranio   You will be schoolmaster
And undertake me teaching of the maid:
That's your device.

Lucentio   It is. May it be done?

Tranio

Not possible; for who shall bear your part
And be in Padua here Vincentio's son,
Keep house and ply his book, welcome his friends,

Visit his countrymen, and banquet them?
Lucentio
    Basta, content thee, for I have it full.
    We have not yet been seen in any house,
    Nor can we be distinguished by our faces
    For man or master. Then it follows thus:
    Thou shalt be master, Tranio, in my stead,
    Keep house, and port, and servants, as I should.
    I will some other be, some Florentine,
    Some Neapolitan, or meaner man of Pisa.
    'Tis hatched and shall be so. Tranio, at once
    Uncase thee. Take my colored hat and cloak.
    When Biondello comes, he waits on thee,
    But I will charm him first to keep his tongue.
Tranio   So had you need.
    In brief, sir, sith it your pleasure is,
    And I am tied to be obedient—
    For so your father charged me at our parting,
    "Be serviceable to my son," quoth he,
    Although I think 'twas in another sense—
    I am content to be Lucentio,
    Because so well I love Lucentio.

                                        [*They exchange clothes.*]

Lucentio
    Tranio, be so, because Lucentio loves.
    And let me be a slave t' achieve that maid
    Whose sudden sight hath thralled my wounded eye.

                    Enter Biondello.

    Here comes the rogue.—Sirrah, where have you been?
Biondello
    Where have I been? Nay, how now, where are you?
    Master, has my fellow Tranio stol'n your clothes?
    Or you stol'n his? Or both? Pray, what's the news?
Lucentio
    Sirrah, come hither. 'Tis no time to jest,

And therefore frame your manners to the time.
Your fellow Tranio here, to save my life,
Puts my apparel and my countenance on,
And I for my escape have put on his;
For in a quarrel since I came ashore,
I killed a man, and fear I was descried.
Wait you on him, I charge you, as becomes,
While I make way from hence to save my life.
You understand me?

Biondello   I, sir?—Ne'er a whit.

Lucentio

And not a jot of Tranio in your mouth.
Tranio is changed into Lucentio.

Biondello

The better for him. Would I were so, too!

Tranio

So could I, faith, boy, to have me next wish after,
That Lucentio indeed had Baptista's youngest daughter.
But, sirrah, not for my sake, but your master's, I advise
You use your manners discreetly in all kind of companies.
When I am alone, why, then I am Tranio,
But in all places else your master Lucentio.

Lucentio   Tranio, let's go.

One thing more rests, that thyself execute:
To make one among these wooers. If thou ask me why,
Sufficeth my reasons are both good and weighty.

[Exeunt.]

The presenters above speak.

First Servingman

My lord, you nod. You do not mind the play.

Sly   Yes, by Saint Anne, do I. A good matter, surely. Comes there any
more of it?

Page [as lady]   My lord, 'tis but begun.

Sly   'Tis a very excellent piece of work, madam lady. Would 'twere
done!   *[They sit and mark.]*

1.2 ENTER PETRUCHIO AND HIS MAN, GRUMIO.

Petruchio

    Verona, for a while I take my leave

    To see my friends in Padua, but of all

    My best belovèd and approvèd friend,

    Hortensio; and I trow this is his house.

    Here, sirrah Grumio, knock, I say.

Grumio   Knock, sir? Whom should I knock? Is there any man has re-

    bused your worship?

Petruchio   Villain, I say, knock me here soundly.

Grumio   Knock you here, sir? Why, sir, what am I, sir, that I should

    knock you here, sir?

Petruchio

    Villain, I say, knock me at this gate,

    And rap me well, or I'll knock your knave's pate.

Grumio

    My master is grown quarrelsome. I should knock you first,

    And then I know after who comes by the worst.

Petruchio   Will it not be?

    Faith, sirrah, an you'll not knock, I'll ring it.

    I'll try how you can *sol fa* and sing it.

                                      [*He wrings him by the ears.*]

Grumio

    Help, masters, help! My master is mad.

Petruchio

    Now knock when I bid you, sirrah villain.

Enter Hortensio.

Hortensio   How now, what's the matter? My old friend Grumio and

    my good friend Petruchio? How do you all at Verona?

Petruchio

    Signor Hortensio, come you to part the fray?

    Con tutto il cuore ben trovato, may I say.

Hortensio

    Alla nostra casa ben venuto,

    Molto onorato signor mio Petruchio.—

Rise, Grumio, rise. We will compound this quarrel.

Grumio Nay, 'tis no matter, sir, what he 'leges in Latin. If this be not
a lawful cause for me to leave his service! Look you, sir: he bid me
knock him and rap him soundly, sir. Well, was it fit for a servant
to use his master so, being perhaps, for aught I see, two-and-thirty,
a pip out?

Whom would to God I had well knocked at first,

Then had not Grumio come by the worst.

Petruchio

> A senseless villain! Good Hortensio,
> I bade the rascal knock upon your gate,
> And could not get him for my heart to do it.

Grumio   Knock at the gate? O heavens! Spake you not these words plain, "Sirrah, knock me here, rap me here, knock me well, and knock me soundly"? And come you now with "knocking at the gate"?

Petruchio

> Sirrah, begone, or talk not, I advise you.

Hortensio

> Petruchio, patience. I am Grumio's pledge.
> Why, this's a heavy chance twixt him and you,
> Your ancient, trusty, pleasant servant Grumio.
> And tell me now, sweet friend, what happy gale
> Blows you to Padua here from old Verona?

Petruchio

> Such wind as scatters young men through the world
> To seek their fortunes farther than at home,
> Where small experience grows. But in a few,
> Signor Hortensio, thus it stands with me:
> Antonio, my father, is deceased,
> And I have thrust myself into this maze,
> Happily to wive and thrive as best I may.
> Crowns in my purse I have, and goods at home,
> And so am come abroad to see the world.

Hortensio

> Petruchio, shall I then come roundly to thee
> And wish thee to a shrewd, ill-favored wife?
> Thou'dst thank me but a little for my counsel.
> And yet I'll promise thee she shall be rich,
> And very rich. But thou'rt too much my friend,
> And I'll not wish thee to her.

Petruchio

> Signor Hortensio, twixt such friends as we
> Few words suffice. And therefore, if thou know

> One rich enough to be Petruchio's wife—
> As wealth is burden of my wooing dance—
> Be she as foul as was Florentius love,
> As old as Sibyl, and as curst and shrewd
> As Socrates' Xanthippe, or a worse,
> She moves me not, or not removes, at least,
> Affection's edge in me, were she as rough
> As are the swelling Adriatic seas.
> I come to wive it wealthily in Padua;
> If wealthily, then happily in Padua.

Grumio   Nay, look you, sir, he tells you flatly what his mind is. Why, give him gold enough and marry him to a puppet or an aglet-baby, or an old trot with ne'er a tooth in her head, though she have as many diseases as two-and-fifty horses. Why, nothing comes amiss, so money comes withal.

Hortensio
> Petruchio, since we are stepped thus far in,
> I will continue that I broached in jest.
> I can, Petruchio, help thee to a wife
> With wealth enough, and young and beauteous,
> Brought up as best becomes a gentlewoman.
> Her only fault, and that is faults enough,
> Is that she is intolerable curst
> And shrewd, and froward, so beyond all measure
> That, were my state far worser than it is,
> I would not wed her for a mine of gold.

Petruchio
> Hortensio, peace! Thou know'st not gold's effect.
> Tell me her father's name and 'tis enough;
> For I will board her, though she chide as loud
> As thunder when the clouds in autumn crack.

Hortensio
> Her father is Baptista Minola,
> An affable and courteous gentleman.
> Her name is Katharina Minola,
> Renowned in Padua for her scolding tongue.

Petruchio

 I know her father, though I know not her,
 And he knew my deceasèd father well.
 I will not sleep, Hortensio, till I see her;
 And therefore let me be thus bold with you
 To give you over at this first encounter,
 Unless you will accompany me thither.

Grumio [*to Hortensio*] I pray you, sir, let him go while the humor lasts. O' my word, an she knew him as well as I do, she would think scolding would do little good upon him. She may perhaps call him half a score knaves or so. Why, that's nothing all the begin once, he'll rail in his rope tricks. I'll tell you what, sir: an she stand him but a little, he will throw a figure in her face and so disfigure her with it that she shall have no more eyes to see withal than a cat. You know him not, sir.

Hortensio

 Tarry, Petruchio, I must go with thee,
 For in Baptista's keep my treasure is.
 He hath the jewel of my life in hold,
 His youngest daughter, beautiful Bianca,
 And her withholds from me and other more,
 Suitors to her and rivals in my love,
 Supposing it a thing impossible,
 For those defects I have before rehearsed,
 That ever Katharina will be wooed.
 Therefore this order hath Baptista ta'en,
 That none shall have access unto Bianca
 Till Katharine the curst have got a husband.

Grumio Katharine the curst!

 A title for a maid of all titles the worst.

Hortensio

 Now shall my friend Petruchio do me grace,
 And offer me disguised in sober robes
 To old Baptista as a schoolmaster
 Well seen in music, to instruct Bianca,
 That so I may by this device at least

Have leave and leisure to make love to her,
And unsuspected court her by herself.

*Enter Gremio [with a paper], and Lucentio disguised
[as a schoolmaster].*

Grumio   Here's no knavery! See, to beguile the old folks, how the
young folks lay their heads together! Master, master, look about
you. Who goes there, ha?
Hortensio
   Peace, Grumio, it is the rival of my love.
   Petruchio, stand by awhile.   [*They stand aside.*]
Grumio   [*aside*]
   A proper stripling and an amorous!
Gremio   [*to Lucentio*]
   O, very well, I have perused the note.
   Hark you, sir, I'll have them very fairly bound—
   All books of love, see that at any hand—
   And see you read no other lectures to her.
   You understand me. Over and besides
   Signor Baptista's liberality,
   I'll mend it with a largess. Take your paper too,
                                   [*giving Lucentio the note*]
   And let me have them very well perfumed,
   For she is sweeter than perfume itself
   To whom they go to. What will you read to her?
Lucentio
   Whate'er I read to her, I'll plead for you
   as for my patron, stand you so assured,
   As firmly as yourself were still in place—
   Yea, and perhaps with more successful words
   Than you, unless you were a scholar, sir.
Gremio
   O this learning, what a thing it is!
Grumio   [*aside*]
   O this woodcock, what an ass it is!
Petruchio   Peace, sirrah!

Hortensio [*coming forward*]

Grumio, mum!—God save you, Signor Gremio.

Gremio

And you are well met, Signor Hortensio.
Trow you whither I am going? To Baptista Minola.
I promised to inquire carefully
About a schoolmaster for the fair Bianca,
And by good fortune I have lighted well
On this young man, for learning and behavior
Fit for her turn, well read in poetry
And other books—good ones, I warrant ye.

Hortensio

'Tis well. And I have met a gentleman
Hath promised me to help me to another,
A fine musician to instruct our mistress.
So shall I no whit be behind in duty
To fair Bianca, so beloved of me.

Gremio

Beloved of me, and that my deeds shall prove.

Grumio [*aside*]   And that his bags shall prove.

Hortensio

Gremio, 'tis now no time to vent our love.
Listen to me, and if you speak me fair,
I'll tell you news indifferent good for either.
Here is a gentleman whom by chance I met,
Upon agreement from us to his liking,
Will undertake to woo curst Katharine,
Yea, and to marry her, if her dowry please.

Gremio   So said, so done, is well.

Hortensio, have you told him all her faults?

Petruchio

I know she is an irksome brawling scold.
If that be all, masters, I hear no harm.

Gremio

No, sayst me so, friend? What countryman?

Petruchio

    Born in Verona, old Antonio's son.

    My father dead, his fortune lives for me,

    And I do hope good days and long to see.

Gremio

    O sir, such a life with such a wife were strange.

    But if you have a stomach, to 't, i' God's name.

    You shall have me assisting you in all.

    But will you woo this wildcat?

Petruchio   Will I live?

Grumio

    Will he woo her? Ay, or I'll hang her.

Petruchio

    Why came I hither but to that intent?

    Think you a little din can daunt mine ears?

    Have I not in my time heard lions roar?

    Have I not heard the sea, puffed up with winds,

    Rage like an angry boar chafèd with sweat?

    Have I not heard great ordnance in the field,

    And heaven's artillery thunder in the skies?

    Have I not in a pitchèd battle heard

    Loud 'larums, neighing steeds, and trumpets' clang?

    And do you tell me of a woman's tongue,

    That gives not half so great a blow to hear

    As will a chestnut in a farmer's fire?

    Tush, tush! Fear boys with bugs.

Grumio   For he fears none.

Gremio   Hortensio, hark.

    This gentleman is happily arrived,

    My mind presumes, for his own good and ours.

Hortensio

    I promised we would be contributors

    And bear his charge of wooing, whatsoe'er.

Gremio

    And so we will, provided that he win her.

Grumio

    I would I were as sure of a good dinner.

         Enter Tranio, brave [as Lucentio], and Biondello.

Tranio

    Gentlemen, God save you. If I may be bold,

    Tell me, I beseech you, which is the readiest way

    To the house of Signor Baptista Minola?

Biondello   He that has the two fair daughters, is 't he you mean?

Tranio   Even he, Biondello.

Gremio

    Hark you, sir, you mean not her to—

Tranio

    Perhaps him and her, sir. What have you to do?

Petruchio

    Not her that chides, sir, at any hand, I pray.

Tranio

    I love no chiders, sir. Biondello, let's away.

Lucentio [aside]

    Well begun, Tranio.

Hortensio   Sir, a word ere you go.

    Are you a suitor to the maid you talk of, yea or no?

Tranio

    An if I be, sir, is it any offense?

Gremio

    No, if without more words you will get you hence.

Tranio

    Why, sir, I pray, are not the streets as free

    For me as for you?

Gremio   But so is not she.

Tranio

    For what reason, I beseech you?

Gremio   For this reason, if you'll know,

    That she's the choice love of Signor Gremio.

Hortensio

    That she's the chosen of Signor Hortensio.

Tranio

    Softly, my masters! If you be gentlemen,
    Do me this right hear me with patience.
    Baptista is a noble gentleman,
    To whom my father is not all unknown;
    And were his daughter fairer than she is,
    She may more suitors have, and me for one.
    Fair Leda's daughter had a thousand wooers;
    Then well one more may fair Bianca have,
    And so she shall. Lucentio shall make one,
    Though Paris came in hope to speed alone.

Gremio

    What, this gentleman will out-talk us all!

Lucentio

    Sir, give him head. I know he'll prove a jade.

Petruchio

    Hortensio, to what end are all these words?

Hortensio [to *Tranio*]

    Sir, let me be so bold as ask you,
    Did you yet ever see Baptista's daughter?

Tranio

    No, sir, but hear I do that he hath two,
    The one as famous for a scolding tongue
    As is the other for beauteous modesty.

Petruchio

    Sir, sir, the first's for me. Let her go by.

Gremio

    Yea, leave that labor to great Hercules,
    And let it be more than Alcides' twelve.

Petruchio

    Sir, understand you this of me, in sooth:
    The youngest daughter, whom you hearken for,
    Her father keeps from all access of suitors,
    And will not promise her to any man
    Until the elder sister first be wed.
    The younger then is free, and not before.

Tranio

    If it be so, sir, that you are the man

    Must stead us all, and me amongst the rest;

    And if you break the ice and do this feat,

    Achieve the elder, set the younger free

    For our access, whose hap shall be to have her

    Will not so graceless be to be ingrate.

Hortensio

    Sir, you say well, and well you do conceive.

    And since you do profess to be a suitor,

    You must, as we do, gratify this gentleman,

    To whom we all rest generally beholding.

Tranio

    Sir, I shall not be slack. In sign whereof,

    Please ye we may contrive this afternoon,

    And quaff carouses to our mistress' health,

    And do as adversaries do in law—

    Strive mightily, but eat and drink as friends.

Grumio, Biondello

    O excellent motion! Fellows, let's be gone.

Hortensio

    The motion's good indeed, and be it so.

    Petruchio, I shall be your *ben venuto*.   [*Exeunt.*]

    2.1 ENTER KATHARINA AND BIANCA [WITH HER HANDS TIED].

Bianca

    Good sister, wrong me not, nor wrong yourself,

    To make a bondmaid and a slave of me.

    That I disdain. But for these other goods,

    Unbind my hands, I'll pull them off myself,

    Yea, all my raiment, to my petticoat,

    Or what you will command me will I do,

    So well I know my duty to my elders.

Katharina

    Of all thy suitors here I charge thee tell

Whom thou lov'st best. See thou dissemble not.

Bianca

Believe me, sister, of all the men alive
I never yet beheld that special face
Which I could fancy more than any other.

Katharina

Minion, thou liest. Is 't not Hortensio?

Bianca

If you affect him, sister, here I swear
I'll plead for you myself but you shall have him.

Katharina

O, then belike you fancy riches more:
You will have Gremio to keep you fair.

Bianca

　　Is it for him you do envy me so?

　　Nay, then, you jest, and now I well perceive

　　You have but jested with me all this while.

　　I prithee, sister Kate, untie my hands.

Katharina [*strikes her*]

　　If that be jest, then all the rest was so.

Enter Baptista.

Baptista

　　Why, how now, dame, whence grows this insolence?—

　　Bianca, stand aside. Poor girl, she weeps.

　　Go ply thy needle, meddle not with her.—

　　For shame, thou hilding of a devilish spirit,

　　Why dost thou wrong her that did ne'er wrong thee?

　　When did she cross thee with a bitter word?

Katharina

Her silence flouts me, and I'll be revenged.

[She] flies after Bianca.

Baptista

What, in my sight? Bianca, get thee in.

Exit [Bianca].

Katharina

What, will you not suffer me? Nay, now I see
She is your treasure, she must have a husband;
I must dance barefoot on her wedding day,
And for your love to her lead apes in hell.
Talk not to me. I will go sit and weep
Till I can find occasion of revenge.   *[Exit.]*

Baptista

Was ever gentleman thus grieved as I?
But who comes here?

*Enter Gremio, Lucentio [as a schoolmaster] in the habit of a mean man,
Petruchio, with [Hortensio as a musician, and] Tranio [as Lucentio]
with his boy [Biondello] bearing a lute and books.*

Gremio   Good morrow, neighbor Baptista.

Baptista   Good morrow, neighbor Gremio. God save you, gentlemen.

Petruchio

And you, good sir. Pray, have you not a daughter
Called Katharina, fair and virtuous?

Baptista

I have a daughter, sir, called Katharina.

Gremio

You are too blunt. Go to it orderly.

Petruchio

You wrong me, Signor Gremio; give me leave.—
I am a gentleman of Verona, sir,
That, hearing of her beauty and her wit,
Her affability and bashful modesty,
Her wondrous qualities and mild behavior,
Am bold to show myself a forward guest

Within your house, to make mine eye the witness
Of that report which I so oft have heard.
And, for an entrance to my entertainment,
I do present you with a man of mine,

[presenting Hortensio]

Cunning in music and the mathematics,
To instruct her fully in those sciences,
Whereof I know she is not ignorant.
Accept of him, or else you do me wrong.
His name is Litio, born in Mantua.

Baptista

You're welcome, sir, and he, for your good sake.
But for my daughter Katharine, this I know,
She is not for your turn, the more my grief.

Petruchio

I see you do not mean to part with her,
Or else you like not of my company.

Baptista

Mistake me not, I speak but as I find.
Whence are you, sir? What may I call your name?

Petruchio

Petruchio is my name, Antonio's son,
A man well known throughout all Italy.

Baptista

I know him well. You are welcome for his sake.

Gremio

Saving your tale, Petruchio, I pray,
Let us that are poor petitioners speak too.
Bacare! You are marvelous forward.

Petruchio

O, pardon me, Signor Gremio, I would fain be doing.

Gremio

I doubt it not, sir, but you will curse your wooing.—Neighbors, this
is a gift very grateful, I am sure of it [*To Baptista.*] To express the
like kindness, myself, that have been more kindly beholding to
you than any, freely give unto you this young scholar [*presenting*

Lucentio], that hath been long studying at Rheims, as cunning in Greek, Latin, and other languages, as the other in music and mathematics. His name is Cambio. Pray, accept his service.

Baptista A thousand thanks, Signor Gremio. Welcome, good Cambio. [*To Tranio.*] But, gentle sir, methinks you walk like a stranger. May I be so bold to know the cause of your coming?

Tranio

Pardon me, sir, the boldness is mine own,

That, being a stranger in this city here,

Do make myself a suitor to your daughter,

Unto Bianca, fair and virtuous.

Nor is your firm resolve unknown to me

In the preferment of the eldest sister.

This liberty is all that I request,

That, upon knowledge of my parentage,

I may have welcome 'mongst the rest that woo,

And free access and favor as the rest.

And toward the education of your daughters

I here bestow a simple instrument,

And this small packet of Greek and Latin books.

If you accept them, then their worth is great.

                    [*Biondello brings forward the lute and books.*]

Baptista

Lucentio is your name? Of whence, I pray?

Tranio

Of Pisa, sir, son to Vincentio.

Baptista

A mighty man of Pisa. By report

I know him well. You are very welcome, sir.

[*To Hortensio.*] Take you the lute, [*to Lucentio*] and you the set of books;

You shall go see your pupils presently.

Holla, within!

Enter a Servant.

Sirrah, lead these gentlemen

To my daughters, and tell them both
These are their tutors. Bid them use them well.

> [*Exit Servant, with Lucentio and Hortensio.*]

We will go walk a little in the orchard,
And then to dinner. You are passing welcome,
And so I pray you all to think yourselves.

Petruchio

Signor Baptista, my business asketh haste,
And every day I cannot come to woo.
You knew my father well, and in him me,
Left solely heir to all his lands and goods,
Which I have bettered rather than decreased.
Then tell me, if I get your daughter's love,
What dowry shall I have with her to wife?

Baptista

After my death the one half of my lands,

And in possession twenty thousand crowns.

Petruchio

And for that dowry I'll assure her of
Her widowhood, be it that she survive me,
In all my lands and leases whatsoever.
Let specialties be therefore drawn between us,
That covenants may be kept on either hand.

Baptista

Ay, when the special thing is well obtained,
That is, her love; for that is all in all.

Petruchio

Why, that is nothing, for I tell you, Father,
I am as peremptory as she proud-minded;
And where two raging fires meet together,
They do consume the thing that feeds their fury.
Though little fire grows great with little wind,
Yet extreme gusts will blow out fire and all.
So I to her, and so she yields to me,
For I am rough and woo not like a babe.

Baptista

Well mayst thou woo, and happy be thy speed!
But be thou armed for some unhappy words.

Petruchio

Ay, to the proof, as mountains are for winds,
That shakes not, though they blow perpetually.

Enter Hortensio [as Litio], with his head broke.

Baptista

How now, my friend, why dost thou look so pale?

Hortensio

For fear, I promise you, if I look pale.

Baptista

What, will my daughter prove a good musician?

Hortensio

I think she'll sooner prove a soldier.
Iron may hold with her, but never lutes.

Baptista

　Why then, thou canst not break her to the lute?

Hortensio

　Why, no, for she hath broke the lute to me.
　I did but tell her she mistook her frets,
　And bowed her hand to teach her fingering,
　When, with a most impatient devilish spirit,
　"Frets, call you these?" quoth she, "I'll fume with them."
　And with that word she struck me on the head,
　And through the instrument my pate made way;
　And there I stood amazèd for a while,
　As on a pillory, looking through the lute,
　While she did call me rascal fiddler
　And twangling Jack, with twenty such vile terms,
　As had she studied to misuse me so.

Petruchio

　Now, by the world, it is a lusty wench!
　I love her ten times more than e'er I did.
　O, how I long to have some chat with her!

Baptista [*to Hortensio*]

　Well, go with me, and be not so discomfited.
　Proceed in practice with my younger daughter;
　She's apt to learn and thankful for good turns.—
　Signor Petruchio, will you go with us,
　Or shall I send my daughter Kate to you?

Petruchio

　I pray you, do.　　　　　　　　　[*Exeunt Manet Petruchio.*]
　　　　　　　I'll attend her here,
　And woo her with some spirit when she comes.
　Say that she rail, why then I'll tell her plain
　She sings as sweetly as a nightingale.
　Say that she frown, I'll say she looks as clear
　As morning roses newly washed with dew.
　Say she be mute and will not speak a word,
　Then I'll commend her volubility
　And say she uttereth piercing eloquence.

If she do bid me pack, I'll give her thanks,
As though she bid me stay by her a week.
If she deny to wed, I'll crave the day
When I shall ask the banns and when be married.
But here she comes; and now, Petruchio, speak.

Enter Katharina.

Good morrow, Kate, for that's your name, I hear.
Katharina
Well have you heard, but something hard of hearing.
They call me Katharine that do talk of me.
Petruchio
You lie, in faith, for you are called plain Kate,
And bonny Kate, and sometimes Kate the curst;
But Kate, the prettiest Kate in Christendom,
Kate of Kate Hall, my superdainty Kate,
For dainties are all Kates, and therefore, Kate,
Take this of me, Kate of my consolation:
Hearing thy mildness praised in every town,
Thy virtues spoke of, and thy beauty sounded,
Yet not so deeply as to thee belongs,
Myself am moved to woo thee for my wife.
Katharina
Moved? In good time! Let him that moved you hither
Remove you hence. I knew you at the first
You were a movable.
Petruchio   Why, what's a movable?
Katharina
A joint stool.
Petruchio   Thou hast hit it. Come, sit on me.
Katharina
Asses are made to bear, and so are you.
Petruchio
Women are made to bear, and so are you.
Katharina
No such jade as you, if me you mean.

Petruchio

>Alas, good Kate, I will not burden thee,
>For knowing thee to be but young and light

Katharina

>Too light for such a swain as you to catch,
>And yet as heavy as my weight should be.

Petruchio

>Should be? Should—buzz!

Katharina   Well ta'en, and like a buzzard.

Petruchio

>O slow-winged turtle, shall a buzzard take thee?

Katharina

>Ay, for a turtle, as he takes a buzzard.

Petruchio

>Come, come, you wasp, i' faith you are too angry.

Katharina

>If I be waspish, best beware my sting.

Petruchio

>My remedy is then to pluck it out

Katharina

>Ay, if the fool could find it where it lies.

Petruchio

>Who knows not where a wasp does wear his sting?
>In his tail.

Katharina   In his tongue.

Petruchio   Whose tongue?

Katharina

>Yours, if you talk of tales, and so farewell.

Petruchio

>What, with my tongue in your tail? Nay, come again.
>Good Kate, I am a gentleman—

Katharina   That I'll try.   [*She strikes him.*]

Petruchio

>I swear I'll cuff you if you strike again.

Katharina   So may you lose your arms.

>If you strike me, you are no gentleman,

And if no gentleman, why then no arms.

Petruchio

A herald, Kate? O, put me in thy books!

Katharina   What is your crest, a coxcomb?

Petruchio

A combless cock, so Kate will be my hen.

Katharina

No cock of mine. You crow too like a craven.

Petruchio

Nay, come, Kate, come. You must not look so sour.

Katharina

It is my fashion when I see a crab.

Petruchio

Why, here's no crab, and therefore look not sour.

Katharina   There is, there is.

Petruchio

Then show it me.

Katharina   Had I a glass, I would.

Petruchio   What, you mean my face?

Katharina   Well aimed of such a young one.

Petruchio

Now, by Saint George, I am too young for you.

Katharina

Yet you are withered.

Petruchio   'Tis with cares.

Katharina   I care not.

Petruchio

Nay, hear you, Kate. In sooth, you scape not so.

Katharina

I chafe you if I tarry. Let me go.

Petruchio

No, not a whit. I find you passing gentle.

'Twas told me you were rough, and coy, and sullen,

And now I find report a very liar,

For thou art pleasant, gamesome, passing courteous,

But slow in speech, yet sweet as springtime flowers.

Thou canst not frown, thou canst not look askance,
Nor bite the lip, as angry wenches will,
Nor hast thou pleasure to be cross in talk;
But thou with mildness entertain'st thy wooers,
With gentle conference, soft and affable.
Why does the world report that Kate doth limp?
O sland'rous world! Kate like the hazel twig
Is straight and slender, and as brown in hue
As hazelnuts, and sweeter than the kernels.
O, let me see thee walk, Thou dost not halt.

Katharina

Go, fool, and whom thou keep'st command.

Petruchio

Did ever Dian so become a grove
As Kate this chamber with her princely gait?
O, be thou Dian, and let her be Kate,
And then let Kate be chaste and Dian sportful!

Katharina

Where did you study all this goodly speech?

Petruchio

It is extempore, from my mother wit.

Katharina

A witty mother! Witless else her son.

Petruchio   Am I not wise?

Katharina   Yes, keep you warm.

Petruchio

Marry, so I mean, sweet Katharine, in thy bed.
And therefore, setting all this chat aside,
Thus in plain terms: your father hath consented
That you shall be my wife; your dowry 'greed on;
And will you, nill you, I will marry you.
Now, Kate, I am a husband for your turn,
For by this light, whereby I see thy beauty—
Thy beauty that doth make me like thee well—
Thou must be married to no man but me.

Enter Baptista, Gremio, [and] Tranio [as Lucentio].

For I am he am born to tame you, Kate,
And bring you from a wild Kate to a Kate
Conformable as other household Kates.
Here comes your father. Never make denial;
I must and will have Katharine to my wife.

Baptista

Now, Signor Petruchio, how speed you with my daughter?

Petruchio

How but well, sir, how but well?
It were impossible I should speed amiss.

Baptista

Why, how now, daughter Katharine, in your dumps?

Katharina

Call you me daughter? Now, I promise you,

You have showed a tender fatherly regard,
To wish me wed to one half-lunatic,
A madcap ruffian and a swearing Jack,
That thinks with oaths to face the matter out.

Petruchio

Father, 'tis thus: yourself and all the world
That talked of her have talked amiss of her.
If she be curst, it is for policy,
For she's not froward, but modest as the dove.
She is not hot, but temperate as the morn.
For patience she will prove a second Grissel,
And Roman Lucrece for her chastity.
And to conclude, we have 'greed so well together
That upon Sunday is the wedding day.

Katharina

I'll see thee hanged on Sunday first.

Gremio   Hark, Petruchio, she says she'll see thee hanged first.

Tranio

Is this your speeding? Nay then, good night our part!

Petruchio

Be patient, gentlemen, I choose her for myself.
If she and I be pleased, what's that to you?
'Tis bargained twixt us twain, being alone,
That she shall still be curst in company.
I tell you, 'tis incredible to believe
How much she loves me. O, the kindest Kate!
She hung about my neck, and kiss on kiss
She vied so fast, protesting oath on oath,
That in a twink she won me to her love.
O, you are novices! 'Tis a world to see
How tame, when men and women are alone,
A meacock wretch can make the curstest shrew.—
Give me thy hand, Kate. I will unto Venice
To buy apparel gainst the wedding day.—
Provide the feast, Father, and bid the guests.

I will be sure my Katharine shall be fine.

Baptista

I know not what to say. But give me your hands.

God send you joy, Petruchio! 'Tis a match.

Gremio, Tranio

Amen, say we. We will be witnesses.

Petruchio

Father, and wife, and gentlemen, adieu.

I will to Venice. Sunday comes apace.

We will have rings, and things, and fine array;

And kiss me, Kate. We will be married o' Sunday.

Exeunt Petruchio and Katharine [separately].

Gremio

Was ever match clapped up so suddenly?

Baptista

Faith, gentlemen, now I play a merchant's part,

And venture madly on a desperate mart.

Tranio

'Twas a commodity lay fretting by you;

'Twill bring you gain, or perish on the seas.

Baptista

The gain I seek is quiet in the match.

Gremio

No doubt but he hath got a quiet catch.

But now, Baptista, to your younger daughter.

Now is the day we long have lookèd for.

I am your neighbor, and was suitor first.

Tranio

And I am one that love Bianca more

Than words can witness, or your thoughts can guess.

Gremio

Youngling, thou canst not love so dear as I.

Tranio

Graybeard, thy love doth freeze.

Gremio   But thine doth fry.

Skipper, stand back. 'Tis age that nourisheth.

Tranio

But youth in ladies' eyes that flourisheth.

Baptista

Content you, gentlemen, I will compound this strife.
'Tis deeds must win the prize, and he of both
That can assure my daughter greatest dower
Shall have my Bianca's love.
Say, Signor Gremio, what can you assure her?

Gremio

First, as you know, my house within the city
Is richly furnished with plate and gold,
Basins and ewers to lave her dainty hands;
My hangings all of Tyrian tapestry;
In ivory coffers I have stuffed my crowns;
In cypress chests my arras counterpoints,
Costly apparel, tents, and canopies,
Fine linen, Turkey cushions bossed with pearl,
Valance of Venice gold in needlework,
Pewter and brass, and all things that belongs
To house or housekeeping. Then at my farm
I have a hundred milch kine to the pail,
Sixscore fat oxen standing in my stalls,
And all things answerable to this portion.
Myself am struck in years, I must confess,
And if I die tomorrow, this is hers,
If whilst I live she will be only mine.

Tranio

That "only" came well in. Sir, list to me:
I am my father's heir and only son.
If I may have your daughter to my wife,
I'll leave her houses three or four as good,
Within rich Pisa walls, as any one
Old Signor Gremio has in Padua,
Besides two thousand ducats by the year
Of fruitful land, all which shall be her jointure.

What, have I pinched you, Signor Gremio?

Gremio

Two thousand ducats by the year of land!

[*Aside.*] My land amounts not to so much in all.—

That she shall have, besides an argosy

That now is lying in Marseilles road.

[*To Tranio.*] What, have I choked you with an argosy?

Tranio

Gremio, 'tis known my father hath no less

Than three great argosies, besides two galliases

And twelve tight galleys. These I will assure her,

And twice as much, whate'er thou off'rest next.

Gremio

Nay, I have offered all. I have no more,

And she can have no more than all I have.

[*To Baptista.*] If you like me, she shall have me and mine.

Tranio

Why then, the maid is mine from all the world,

By your firm promise. Gremio is outvied.

Baptista

I must confess your offer is the best;

And, let your father make her the assurance,

She is your own; else, you must pardon me.

If you should die before him, where's her dower?

Tranio

That's but a cavil. He is old, I young.

Gremio

And may not young men die, as well as old?

Baptista

Well, gentlemen, I am thus resolved:

On Sunday next, you know

My daughter Katharine is to be married.

Now, on the Sunday following shall Bianca

Be bride [*to Tranio*] to you, if you make this assurance;

If not, to Signer Gremio.

And so I take my leave, and thank you both.   [*Exit.*]

Gremio

    Adieu, good neighbor.—Now I fear thee not.

    Sirrah, young gamester, your father were a fool

    To give thee all, and in his waning age

    Set foot under thy table. Tut, a toy!

    An old Italian fox is not so kind, my boy.   [*Exit.*]

Tranio

    A vengeance on your crafty withered hide!

    Yet I have faced it with a card of ten.

    'Tis in my head to do my master good.

    I see no reason but supposed Lucentio

    Must get a father, called supposed Vincentio—

    And that's a wonder. Fathers commonly

    Do get their children; but in this case of wooing,

    A child shall get a sire, if I fail not of my cunning.   [*Exit.*]

3.1 ENTER LUCENTIO [AS CAMBIO], HORTENSIO [AS LITIO],
AND BIANCA.

Lucentio

    Fiddler, forbear. You grow too forward, sir.

    Have you so soon forgot the entertainment

    Her sister Katharine welcomed you withal?

Hortensio

    But, wrangling pedant, this is

    The patroness of heavenly harmony.

    Then give me leave to have prerogative,

    And when in music we have spent an hour,

    Your lecture shall have leisure for as much.

Lucentio

    Preposterous ass, that never read so far

    To know the cause why music was ordained!

    Was it not to refresh the mind of man

    After his studies or his usual pain?

    Then give me leave to read philosophy,

    And, while I pause, serve in your harmony.

Hortensio
    Sirrah, I will not bear these braves of thine.
Bianca
    Why, gentlemen, you do me double wrong
    To strive for that which resteth in my choice.
    I am no breeching scholar in the schools;

I'll not be tied to hours nor 'pointed times,
But learn my lessons as I please myself.
And, to cut off all strife, here sit we down.
[*To Hortensio.*] Take you your instrument, play you the whiles;
His lecture will be done ere you have tuned.

Hortensio
You'll leave his lecture when I am in tune?

Lucentio
That will be never. Tune your instrument.

> [*Hortensio moves aside and tunes.*]

Bianca   Where left we last?

Lucentio   Here, madam. [*He reads.*]
"Hic ibat Simois; hic est Sigeia tellus;
Hic steterat Priami regia celsa senis."

Bianca   Conster them.

Lucentio   "Hic ibat," as I told you before, "Simois," I am Lucentio, "hic
est," son unto Vincentio of Pisa, "Sigeia tellus," disguised thus to get
your love; "Hic steterat," and that Lucentio that comes a-wooing,
"Priami," is my man Tranio, "regia," bearing my port, "celsa senis,"
that we might beguile the old pantaloon.

Hortensio   Madam, my instrument's in tune.

Bianca   Let's hear. [*He plays.*] O fie! The treble jars.

Lucentio   Spit in the hole, man, and tune again.

> [*Hortensio moves aside.*]

Bianca   Now let me see if I can conster it: "Hic ibat Simois," I know
you not, "hic est Sigeia tellus," I trust you not; "Hic steterat Priami,"
take heed he hear us not, "regia," presume not, "celsa senis," despair
not.

Hortensio
Madam, 'tis now in tune.   [*He plays again.*]

Lucentio   All but the bass.

Hortensio
The bass is right, 'tis the base knave that jars.
[*Aside.*] How fiery and forward our pedant is!
Now, for my life, the knave doth court my love.
Pedascule, I'll watch you better yet.

Bianca [*to Lucentio*]
> In time I may believe, yet I mistrust.

Lucentio
> Mistrust it not, for, sure, Aeacides
> Was Ajax, called so from his grandfather.

Bianca
> I must believe my master; else, I promise you,
> I should be arguing still upon that doubt.
> But let it rest.—Now, Litio, to you:
> Good master, take it not unkindly, pray,
> That I have been thus pleasant with you both.

Hortensio [*to Lucentio*]
> You may go walk, and give me leave awhile.
> My lessons make no music in three parts.

Lucentio
> Are you so formal, sir? Well, I must wait.
> [*Aside.*] And watch withal; for, but I be deceived,
> Our fine musician groweth amorous.

> > > > > [*He moves aside.*]

Hortensio
> Madam, before you touch the instrument,
> To learn the order of my fingering,
> I must begin with rudiments of art,
> To teach you gamut in a briefer sort,
> More pleasant, pithy, and effectual
> Than hath been taught by any of my trade.
> And there it is in writing, fairly drawn.

> > > > > [*He gives her a paper.*]

Bianca
> Why, I am past my gamut long ago.

Hortensio
> Yet read the gamut of Hortensio.

Bianca [*reads*]
> "*Gamut* I am, the ground of all accord,
> A *re*, to plead Hortensio's passion;
> B *mi*, Bianca, take him for thy lord,

C *fa ut*, that loves with all affection.
D *sol re*, one clef, two notes have I;
E *la mi*, show pity, or I die."
Call you this gamut? Tut, I like it not.
Old fashions please me best; I am not so nice
To change true rules for odd inventions.

Enter a [Servant as] messenger.

Servant

    Mistress, your father prays you leave your books
    And help to dress your sister's chamber up.
    You know tomorrow is the wedding day.

Bianca

    Farewell, sweet masters both. I must be gone.

Lucentio

    Faith, mistress, then I have no cause to stay.

        [Exeunt Bianca, Servant, and Lucentio.]

Hortensio

    But I have cause to pry into this pedant.
    Methinks he looks as though he were in love.
    Yet if thy thoughts, Bianca, be so humble
    To cast thy wandering eyes on every stale,
    Seize thee that list. If once I find thee ranging,
    Hortensio will be quit with thee by changing.   *[Exit.]*

3.2 ENTER BAPTISTA, GREMIO, TRANIO [AS LUCENTIO],
KATHARINE, BIANCA, LUCENTIO [AS CAMBIO],
AND OTHERS, ATTENDANTS.

Baptista *[to Tranio]*

    Signor Lucentio, this is the 'pointed day
    That Katharine and Petruchio should be married,
    And yet we hear not of our son-in-law.
    What will be said? What mockery will it be,
    To want the bridegroom when the priest attends
    To speak the ceremonial rites of marriage?

What says Lucentio to this shame of ours?

Katharina

No shame but mine. I must, forsooth, be forced
To give my hand opposed against my heart
Unto a mad-brain rudesby full of spleen,
Who wooed in haste and means to wed at leisure.
I told you, I, he was a frantic fool,
Hiding his bitter jests in blunt behavior.
And, to be noted for a merry man,
He'll woo a thousand, 'point the day of marriage,
Make friends, invite, and proclaim the banns,
Yet never means to wed where he hath wooed.
Now must the world point at poor Katharine
And say, "Lo, there is mad Petruchio's wife,
If it would please him come and marry her!"

Tranio

Patience, good Katharine, and Baptista, too.
Upon my life, Petruchio means but well,
Whatever fortune stays him from his word.
Though he be blunt, I know him passing wise;
Though he be merry, yet withal he's honest.

Katharina

Would Katharine had never seen him though!

[*Exit weeping.*]

Baptista

Go, girl, I cannot blame thee now to weep,
For such an injury would vex a very saint,
Much more a shrew of thy impatient humor.

Enter Biondello.

Biondello   Master, master! News, and such old news as you never heard of!

Baptista   Is it new and old too? How may that be?

Biondello   Why, is it not news to hear of Petruchio's coming?

Baptista   Is he come?

Biondello   Why, no, sir.

Baptista   What, then?

Biondello   He is coming.

Baptista   When will he be here?

Biondello   When he stands where I am and sees you there.

Tranio   But say, what to thine old news?

Biondello   Why, Petruchio is coming in a new hat and an old jerkin;
    a pair of old breeches thrice turned; a pair of boots that have been
    candle-cases, one buckled, another laced; an old rusty sword ta'en
    out of the town armory, with a broken hilt, and chapeless; with

two broken points; his horse hipped, with an old mothy saddle and stirrups of no kindred; besides, possessed with the glanders and like to mose in the chine, troubled with the lampass, infected with the fashions, full of windgalls, sped with spavins, rayed with the yellows, past cure of me fives, stark spoiled with the staggers, begnawn with the bots, swayed in the back and shoulder-shotten; near-legged before, and with a half-cheeked bit and a headstall of sheep's leather which, being restrained to keep him from stumbling, hath been often burst and now repaired with knots; one girth six times pieced, and a woman's crupper of velour, which hath two letters for her name fairly set down in studs, and here and there pieced with packthread.

Baptista   Who comes with him?

Biondello   O, sir, his lackey, for all the world caparisoned like the horse; with a linen stock on one leg and a kersey boot-hose on the other, gartered with a red and blue list; an old hat, and the humor of forty fancies pricked in 't for a feather—a monster, a very monster in apparel, and not like a Christian footboy or a gentleman's lackey.

Tranio

'Tis some odd humor pricks him to this fashion;
Yet oftentimes he goes but mean-appareled.

Baptista   I am glad he's come, howsoe'er he comes.

Biondello   Why, sir, he comes not.

Baptista   Didst thou not say he comes?

Biondello   Who? That Petruchio came?

Baptista   Ay, that Petruchio came.

Biondello   No, sir, I say his horse comes, with him on his back.

Baptista   Why, that's all one.

Biondello

Nay, by Saint Jamy,
I hold you a penny,
A horse and a man
Is more than one,
And yet not many.

Enter Petruchio and Grumio.

Petruchio

    Come, where be these gallants? Who's at home?

Baptista   You are welcome, sir.

Petruchio   And yet I come not well

Baptista   And yet you halt not.

Tranio

    Not so well appareled as I wish you were.

Petruchio

    Were it better, I should rush in thus.

    But where is Kate? Where is my lovely bride?

    How does my father? Gentles, methinks you frown.

    And wherefore gaze this goodly company,

    As if they saw some wondrous monument,

    Some comet, or unusual prodigy?

Baptista

    Why, sir, you know this is your wedding day.

    First were we sad, fearing you would not come,

    Now sadder that you come so unprovided.

    Fie, doff this habit, shame to your estate,

    An eyesore to our solemn festival!

Tranio

    And tell us, what occasion of import

    Hath all so long detained you from your wife

    And sent you hither so unlike yourself?

Petruchio

    Tedious it were to tell, and harsh to hear.

    Sufficeth I am come to keep my word,

    Though in some part enforcèd to digress,

    Which at more leisure I will so excuse

    As you shall well be satisfied withal.

    But where is Kate? I stay too long from her.

    The morning wears; 'tis time we were at church.

Tranio

    See not your bride in these unreverent robes.

    Go to my chamber. Put on clothes of mine.

Petruchio

Not I, believe me. Thus I'll visit her.

Baptista

But thus, I trust, you will not marry her.

Petruchio

Good sooth, even thus. Therefore ha' done with words.

To me she's married, not unto my clothes.

Could I repair what she will wear in me

As I can change these poor accoutrements,

'Twere well for Kate and better for myself.

But what a fool am I to chat with you,

When I should bid good morrow to my bride

And seal the title with a lovely kiss!   [*Exit.*]

Tranio

He hath some meaning in his mad attire.

We will persuade him, be it possible,

To put on better ere he go to church.

Baptista

I'll after him, and see the event of this.

                              Exit [*with all but Tranio and Lucentio*].

Tranio

But, sir, to love concerneth us to add

Her father's liking, which to bring to pass,

As I before imparted to your worship,

I am to get a man—whate'er he be

It skills not much, we'll fit him to our turn—

And he shall be Vincentio of Pisa

And make assurance here in Padua

Of greater sums than I have promisèd.

So shall you quietly enjoy your hope

And marry sweet Bianca with consent.

Lucentio

Were it not that my fellow schoolmaster

Doth watch Bianca's steps so narrowly,

'Twere good, methinks, to steal our marriage,

Which once performed, let all the world say no,

I'll keep mine own, despite of all the world.
Tranio
    That by degrees we mean to look into,
    And watch our vantage in this business.
    We'll overreach the graybeard, Gremio,
    The narrow-prying father, Minola,
    The quaint musician, amorous Litio,
    All for my master's sake, Lucentio.

Enter Gremio.

    Signor Gremio, came you from the church?
Gremio
    As willingly as e'er I came from school.
Tranio
    And is the bride and bridegroom coming home?
Gremio
    A bridegroom, say you? 'Tis a groom indeed,
    A grumbling groom, and that the girl shall find.
Tranio
    Curster than she? Why, 'tis impossible.
Gremio
    Why, he's a devil, a devil, a very fiend.
Tranio
    Why, she's a devil, a devil, the devil's dam.
Gremio
    Tut, she's a lamb, a dove, a fool to him.
    I'll tell you, Sir Lucentio. When the priest
    Should ask if Katharine should be his wife,
    "Ay, by Gog's wouns," quoth he, and swore so loud
    That all amazed the priest let fall the book,
    And as he stooped again to take it up,
    This mad-brained bridegroom took him such a cuff
    That down fell priest and book, and book and priest.
    "Now take them up," quoth he, "if any list."
Tranio
    What said the wench when he rose again?

Gremio

    Trembled and shook, forwhy he stamped and swore
    As if the vicar meant to cozen him.
    But after many ceremonies done
    He calls for wine. "A health!" quoth he, as if
    He had been aboard, carousing to his mates
    After a storm; quaffed off the muscatel
    And threw the sops all in the sexton's face,
    Having no other reason
    But that his beard grew thin and hungerly
    And seemed to ask him sops as he was drinking.
    This done, he took the bride about the neck
    And kissed her lips with such a clamorous smack
    That at the parting all the church did echo.
    And I seeing this came thence for very shame,
    And after me, I know, the rout is coming.
    Such a mad marriage never was before.   *Music plays.*
    Hark, hark! I hear the minstrels play.

       Enter Petruchio, Kate, Bianca, Hortensio [as Litio],
           Baptista, [with Grumio, and train].

Petruchio

    Gentlemen and friends, I thank you for your pains.
    I know you think to dine with me today,
    And have prepared great store of wedding cheer;
    But so it is my haste doth call me hence,
    And therefore here I mean to take my leave.

Baptista

    Is 't possible you will away tonight?

Petruchio

    I must away today, before night come.
    Make it no wonder, if you knew my business,
    You would entreat me rather go than stay.
    And, honest company, I thank you all
    That have beheld me give away myself
    To this most patient, sweet, and virtuous wife.

Dine with my father, drink a health to me,
For I must hence; and farewell to you all.

Tranio

Let us entreat you stay till after dinner.

Petruchio

It may not be.

Gremio   Let me entreat you.

Petruchio

It cannot be.

Katharina   Let me entreat you.

Petruchio

I am content.

Katharina   Are you content to stay?

Petruchio

I am content you shall entreat me stay;
But yet not stay, entreat me how you can.

Katharina

Now, if you love me, stay.

Petruchio   Grumio, my horse.

Grumio   Ay, sir, they be ready. The oats have eaten the horses.

Katharina   Nay, then,

Do what thou canst, I will not go today,
No, nor tomorrow—not till I please myself.
The door is open, sir, there lies your way.
You may be jogging whiles your boots are green.
For me, I'll not be gone till I please myself.
'Tis like you'll prove a jolly, surly groom,
That take it on you at the first so roundly.

Petruchio

O Kate, content thee. Prithee, be not angry.

Katharina

I will be angry. What hast thou to do?—
Father, be quiet. He shall stay my leisure.

Gremio

Ay, marry, sir, now it begins to work.

Katharina

Gentlemen, forward to the bridal dinner.
I see a woman may be made a fool
If she had not a spirit to resist.

Petruchio

They shall go forward, Kate, at thy command.—
Obey the bride, you that attend on her.
Go to the feast, revel and domineer,
Carouse full measure to her maidenhead,
Be mad and merry, or go hang yourselves.
But for my bonny Kate, she must with me.
Nay, look not big, nor stamp, nor stare, nor fret;
I will be master of what is mine own.
She is my goods, my chattels; she is my house,
My household stuff, my field, my barn,
My horse, my ox, my ass, my anything;
And here she stands, touch her whoever dare.
I'll bring mine action on the proudest he
That stops my way in Padua.—Grumio,
Draw forth thy weapon. We are beset with thieves.
Rescue thy mistress, if thou be a man.—
Fear not, sweet wench, they shall not touch thee, Kate!
I'll buckler thee against a million.

Exeunt Petruchio, Katharina, [and Grumio].

Baptista

Nay, let them go—a couple of quiet ones!

Gremio

Went they not quickly, I should die with laughing.

Tranio

Of all mad matches never was the like.

Lucentio

Mistress, what's your opinion of your sister?

Bianca

That, being mad herself, she's madly mated.

Gremio

I warrant him, Petruchio is Kated.

Baptista
 Neighbors and friends, though bride and bridegroom wants
 For to supply the places at the table,
 You know there wants no junkets at the feast.
 Lucentio, you shall supply the bridegroom's place,
 And let Bianca take her sister's room.
Tranio
 Shall sweet Bianca practice how to bride it?
Baptista
 She shall, Lucentio. Come, gentlemen, let's go.

[*Exeunt.*]

4.1 ENTER GRUMIO.

Grumio   Fie, fie on all tired jades, on all mad masters, and all foul
 ways! Was ever man so beaten? Was ever man so rayed? Was ever
 man so weary? I am sent before to make a fire, and they are coming
 after to warm them. Now, were not I a little pot and soon hot, my
 very lips might freeze to my teeth, my tongue to the roof of my
 mouth, my heart in my belly, ere I should come by a fire to thaw
 me. But I with blowing the fire shall warm myself; for, considering
 the weather, a taller man than I will take cold. Holla, ho! Curtis!

Enter Curtis.

Curtis   Who is that calls so coldly?
Grumio   A piece of ice. If thou doubt it, thou mayst slide from my
 shoulder to my heel with no greater a run but my head and my
 neck. A fire, good Curtis!
Curtis   Is my master and his wife coming, Grumio?
Grumio   O, ay, Curtis, ay, and therefore fire, fire! Cast on no water.
Curtis   Is she so hot a shrew as she's reported?
Grumio   She was, good Curtis, before this frost. But, thou know'st,
 winter tames man, woman, and beast; for it hath tamed my old
 master and my new mistress and myself, fellow Curtis.
Curtis   Away, you three-inch fool! I am no beast.

Grumio Am I but three inches? Why, thy horn is a foot, and so long am I, at the least. But wilt thou make a fire, or shall I complain on thee to our mistress, whose hand—she being now at hand— thou shalt soon feel, to thy cold comfort, for being slow in thy hot office?

Curtis I prithee, good Grumio, tell me, how goes the world?

Grumio A cold world, Curtis, in every office but thine, and therefore fire. Do thy duty, and have thy duty, for my master and mistress are almost frozen to death.

Curtis There's fire ready, and therefore, good Grumio, the news.

Grumio Why, "Jack boy, ho, boy!" and as much news as wilt thou.

Curtis Come, you are so full of coney-catching.

Grumio Why, therefore fire, for I have caught extreme cold. Where's the cook? Is supper ready, the house trimmed, rushes strewed, cobwebs swept, the servingmen in their new fustian, the white stockings, and every officer his wedding garment on? Be the Jacks fair within, the Jills fair without, the carpets laid, and everything in order?

Curtis   All ready; and therefore, I pray thee, news.

Grumio   First, know my horse is tired, my master and mistress fallen out.

Curtis   How?

Grumio   Out of their saddles into the dirt—and thereby hangs a tale.

Curtis   Let's ha 't, good Grumio.

Grumio   Lend thine ear.

Curtis   Here.

Grumio   There.   [*He cuffs Curtis.*]

Curtis   This 'tis to feel a tale, not to hear a tale.

Grumio   And therefore 'tis called a sensible tale, and this cuff was but to knock at your ear and beseech listening. Now I begin: Imprimis, we came down a foul hill, my master riding behind my mistress—

Curtis   Both of one horse?

Grumio   What's that to thee?

Curtis   Why, a horse.

Grumio   Tell thou the tale. But hadst thou not crossed me, thou shouldst have heard how her horse fell and she under her horse; thou shouldst have heard in how miry a place, how she was bemoiled, how he left her with the horse upon her, how he beat me because her horse stumbled, how she waded through the dirt to pluck him off me, how he swore, how she prayed that never prayed before, how I cried, how the horses ran away, how her bridle was burst, how I lost my crupper, with many things of worthy memory, which now shall die in oblivion and thou return unexperienced to thy grave.

Curtis   By this reckoning he is more shrew than she.

Grumio   Ay, and that thou and the proudest of you all shall find when he comes home. But what talk I of this? Call forth Nathaniel, Joseph, Nicholas, Philip, Walter, Sugarsop, and the rest. Let their heads be sleekly combed, their blue coats brushed, and their garters of an indifferent knit; let them curtsy with their a left legs, and not presume to touch a hair of my master's horsetail till they kiss their hands. Are they all ready?

Curtis   They are.

Grumio   Call them forth.

Curtis [*calling*]   Do you hear, ho? You must meet my master to countenance my mistress.

Grumio   Why, she hath a face of her own.

Curtis   Who knows not that?

Grumio   Thou, it seems, that calls for company to countenance her.

Curtis   I call them forth to credit her.

Enter four or five Servingmen.

Grumio   Why she comes to borrow nothing of them

Nathaniel   Welcome home, Grumio!

Philip   How now, Grumio?

Joseph   What, Grumio!

Nicholas   Fellow Grumio!

Nathaniel   How now, old lad?

Grumio   Welcome, you; how now, you; what, you; fellow, you—and thus much for greeting. Now, my spruce companions, is all ready, and all things neat?

Nathaniel   All things is ready. How near is our master?

Grumio   E'en at hand, alighted by this; and therefore be not—Cock's passion, silence! I hear my master.

Enter Petruchio and Kate.

Petruchio

Where be these knaves? What, no man at door
To hold my stirrup nor to take my horse?
Where is Nathaniel, Gregory, Philip?

All Servants   Here, here, sir, here, sir.

Petruchio

Here, sir! Here, sir! Here, sir! Here, sir!
You loggerheaded and unpolished grooms!
What, no attendance? No regard? No duty?
Where is the foolish knave I sent before?

Grumio

Here, sir, as foolish as I was before.

Petruchio

You peasant swain, you whoreson, malt-horse drudge!
Did I not bid thee meet me in the park
And bring along these rascal knaves with thee?

Grumio

Nathaniel's coat, sir, was not fully made,
And Gabriel's pumps were all unpinked i' the heel.
There was no link to color Peter's hat,
And Walter's dagger was not come from sheathing.
There were none fine but Adam, Ralph, and Gregory;
The rest were ragged, old, and beggarly.
Yet, as they are, here are they come to meet you.

Petruchio

Go, rascals, go and fetch my supper in.

[*Exeunt Servants.*]

[*He sings.*] "Where is the life that late I led?
Where are those—" Sit down, Kate, and welcome.—

> [*They sit at table.*]

Soud, soud, soud, soud!

Enter Servants with supper.

Why, when, I say?— Nay, good sweet Kate, be merry.—
Off with my boots, you rogues! You villains, when?

> [*A Servant takes off Petruchio's boots.*]

[*He sings.*] "It was the friar of orders gray,
        As he forth walked on his way—"
Out, you rogue! You pluck my foot awry.

> [*He kicks the Servant.*]

Take that, and mend the plucking of the other.
Be merry, Kate.—Some water, here. What, ho!

Enter one with water.

Where's my spaniel Troilus? Sirrah, get you hence,
And bid my cousin Ferdinand come hither—

> [*Exit Servant.*]

One, Kate, that you must kiss and be acquainted with.
Where are my slippers? Shall I have some water?
Come, Kate, and wash, and welcome heartily.

> [*A Servant offers water, but spills some.*]

You whoreson villain, will you let it fall?

> [*He strikes the Servant.*]

Katharina
    Patience, I pray you, 'twas a fault unwilling.
Petruchio
    A whoreson, beetleheaded, flap-eared knave!—
    Come, Kate, sit down. I know you have a stomach.
    Will you give thanks, sweet Kate, or else shall I?—
    What's this? Mutton?
First Servant   Ay.
Petruchio   Who brought it?
Peter   I.

Petruchio

    'Tis burnt, and so is all the meat.

    What dogs are these? Where is the rascal cook?

    How durst you, villains, bring it from the dresser

    And serve it thus to me that love it not?

    There, take it to you, trenchers, cups, and all.

                       [He throws the meat, etc., at them.]

    You heedless jolt-heads and unmannered slaves!

    What, do you grumble? I'll be with you straight.

                              [They run out.]

Katharina

    I pray you, husband, be not so disquiet.

    The meat was well, if you were so contented.

Petruchio

    I tell thee, Kate, 'twas burnt and dried away,

    And I expressly am forbid to touch it;

    For it engenders choler, planteth anger,

    And better 'twere that both of us did fast,

    Since, of ourselves, ourselves are choleric,

Than feed it with such overroasted flesh.
Be patient Tomorrow 't shall be mended,
And for this night we'll fast for company.
Come, I will bring thee to thy bridal chamber.

[*Exeunt.*]

Enter Servants severally.

Nathaniel   Peter, didst ever see the like?
Peter   He kills her in her own humor.

Enter Curtis.

Grumio   Where is he?
Curtis   In her chamber,
Making a sermon of continency to her,
And rails, and swears, and rates, that she, poor soul,
Knows not which way to stand, to look, to speak,
And sits as one new risen from a dream.
Away, away! For he is coming hither.

[*Exeunt.*]

Enter Petruchio.

Petruchio
Thus have I politicly begun my reign,
And 'tis my hope to end successfully.
My falcon now is sharp and passing empty,
And till she stoop she must not be full-gorged,
For then she never looks upon her lure.
Another way I have to man my haggard,
To make her come and know her keeper's call:
That is, to watch her, as we watch these kites
That bate and beat and will not be obedient.
She ate no meat today, nor none shall eat.
Last night she slept not, nor tonight she shall not.
As with the meat, some undeservèd fault
I'll find about the making of the bed,
And here I'll fling the pillow, there the bolster,
This way the coverlet, another way the sheets.
Ay, and amid this hurly I intend

That all is done in reverent care of her.
And in conclusion she shall watch all night,
And if she chance to nod I'll rail and brawl,
And with the clamor keep her still awake.
This is a way to kill a wife with kindness;
And thus I'll curb her mad and headstrong humor.
He that knows better how to tame a shrew,
Now let him speak. 'Tis charity to show.   [*Exit.*]

4.2 ENTER TRANIO [AS LUCENTIO] AND HORTENSIO [AS LITIO]

Tranio

Is 't possible, friend Litio, that Mistress Bianca
Doth fancy any other but Lucentio?
I tell you, sir, she bears me fair in hand.

Hortensio

Sir, to satisfy you in what I have said,
Stand by and mark the manner of his teaching.

[*They stand aside.*]

Enter Bianca [*and Lucentio as Cambio*].

Lucentio

Now, mistress, profit you in what you read?

Bianca

What, master, read you? First resolve me that.

Lucentio

I read that I profess, *The Art to Love.*

Bianca

And may you prove, sir, master of your art!

Lucentio

While you, sweet dear, prove mistress of my heart!

[*They move aside and court each other.*]

Hortensio [*to Tranio, coming forward*]

Quick proceeders, marry! Now, tell me, I pray,
You that durst swear that your mistress Bianca

Loved none in the world so well as Lucentio.
Tranio
    O despiteful love! Unconstant womankind!
    I tell thee, Litio, this is wonderful.
Hortensio
    Mistake no more. I am not Litio,
    Nor a musician, as I seem to be,
    But one that scorn to live in this disguise
    For such a one as leaves a gentleman
    And makes a god of such a cullion.
    Know, sir, that I am called Hortensio.
Tranio
    Signor Hortensio, I have often heard
    Of your entire affection to Bianca;
    And since mine eyes are witness of her lightness,
    I will with you, if you be so contented,
    Forswear Bianca and her love forever.

Hortensio

    See how they kiss and court! Signor Lucentio,

    Here is my hand, and here I firmly vow

                                                  [giving his hand]

    Never to woo her more, but do forswear her,

    As one unworthy all the former favors

    That I have fondly flattered her withal

Tranio

    And here I take the like unfeignèd oath,

    Never to marry with her though she would entreat.

    Fie on her, see how beastly she doth court him!

Hortensio

    Would all the world but he had quite forsworn!

    For me, that I may surely keep mine oath,

    I will be married to a wealthy widow,

    Ere three days pass, which hath, as long loved me

    As I have loved this proud disdainful haggard.

    And so farewell, Signor Lucentio.

    Kindness in women, not their beauteous looks,

    Shall win my love. And so I take my leave,

    In resolution as I swore before.   *[Exit.]*

Tranio [as Lucentio and Bianca come forward again]

    Mistress Bianca, bless you with such grace

    As 'longeth to a lover's blessèd case!

    Nay, I have ta'en you napping, gentle love,

    And have forsworn you with Hortensio.

Bianca

    Tranio, you jest. But have you both forsworn me?

Tranio

    Mistress, we have.

Lucentio   Then we are rid of Litio.

Tranio

    I' faith, he'll have a lusty widow now,

    That shall be wooed and wedded in a day.

Bianca   God give him joy!

Tranio   Ay, and he'll tame her.

Bianca   He says so, Tranio?

Tranio

Faith, he is gone unto the taming-school.

Bianca

The taming-school! What, is there such a place?

Tranio

Ay, mistress, and Petruchio is the master,

That teacheth tricks eleven-and-twenty long

To tame a shrew and charm her chattering tongue.

Enter Biondello.

Biondello

O master, master, I have watched so long

That I am dog-weary, but at last I spied

An ancient angel coming down the hill

Will serve the turn.

Tranio   What is he, Biondello?

Biondello

Master, a marcantant, or a pedant,

I know not what, but formal in apparel,

In gait and countenance surely like a father.

Lucentio   And what of him, Tranio?

Tranio

If he be credulous and trust my tale,

I'll make him glad to seem Vincentio,

And give assurance to Baptista Minola

As if he were the right Vincentio.

Take in your love, and then let me alone.

                              [*Exeunt Lucentio mid Bianca.*]

Enter a Pedant.

Pedant

God save you, sir!

Tranio   And you sir! You are welcome.

Travel you far on, or are you at the farthest?

Pedant

    Sir, at the farthest for a week or two,

    But then up farther, and as far as Rome,

    And so to Tripoli, if God lend me life.

Tranio

    What countryman, I pray?

Pedant   Of Mantua.

Tranio

    Of Mantua, sir? Marry, God forbid!

    And come to Padua, careless of your life?

Pedant

    My life, sir? How, I pray? For that goes hard.

Tranio

    'Tis death for anyone in Mantua

    To come to Padua. Know you not the cause?

    Your ships are stayed at Venice, and the Duke,

    For private quarrel twixt your Duke and him,

    Hath published and proclaimed it openly.

    'Tis marvel, but that you are but newly come,

    You might have heard it else proclaimed about.

Pedant

    Alas, sir, it is worse for me than so,

    For I have bills for money by exchange

    From Florence, and must here deliver them.

Tranio

    Well, sir, to do you courtesy,

    This will I do, and this I will advise you—

    First, tell me, have you ever been at Pisa?

Pedant

    Ay, sir, in Pisa have I often been,

    Pisa renownèd for grave citizens.

Tranio

    Among them know you one Vincentio?

Pedant

    I know him not, but I have heard of him;

    A merchant of incomparable wealth.

Tranio

 He is my father, sir, and, sooth to say,

 In count'nance somewhat doth resemble you

Biondello [*aside*]   As much as an apple doth an oyster, and all one.

Tranio

 To save your life in this extremity,

 This favor will I do you for his sake;

 And think it not the worst of all your fortunes

 That you are like to Sir Vincentio.

 His name and credit shall you undertake,

 And in my house you shall be friendly lodged.

 Look that you take upon you as you should.

 You understand me, sir. So shall you stay

 Till you have done your business in the city.

 If this be courtesy, sir, accept of it.

Pedant

 O sir, I do, and will repute you ever

 The patron of my life and liberty.

Tranio

 Then go with me to make the matter good.

 This, by the way, I let you understand:

 My father is here looked for every day

 To pass assurance of a dower in marriage

 Twixt me and one Baptista's daughter here.

 In all these circumstances I'll instruct you.

 Go with me to clothe you as becomes you

               [*Exeunt.*]

4.3 ENTER KATHARINA AND GRUMIO.

Grumio

 No, no, forsooth, I dare not for my life.

Katharina

 The more my wrong, the more his spite appears.

 What, did he marry me to famish me?

 Beggars that come unto my father's door

Upon entreaty have a present alms;
If not, elsewhere they meet with charity.
But I, who never knew how to entreat,
Nor never needed that I should entreat,
Am starved for meat, giddy for lack of sleep,
With oaths kept waking, and with brawling fed.
And that which spites me more than all these wants,
He does it under name of perfect love,
As who should say, if I should sleep or eat
'Twere deadly sickness or else present death.
I prithee, go and get me some repast,
I care not what, so it be wholesome food.

Grumio   What say you to a neat's foot?

Katharina

'Tis passing good. I prithee, let me have it.

Grumio

I fear it is too choleric a meat.

How say you to a fat tripe finely broiled?

Katharina

I like it well. Good Grumio, fetch it me.

Grumio

I cannot tell. I fear 'tis choleric.

What say you to a piece of beef and mustard?

Katharina

A dish that I do love to feed upon.

Grumio

Ay, but the mustard is too hot a little.

Katharina

Why then, the beef, and let the mustard rest.

Grumio

Nay then, I will not. You shall have the mustard,
Or else you get no beef of Grumio.

Katharina

Then both, or one, or anything thou wilt.

Grumio

Why then, the mustard without the beef.

Katharina

Go, get thee gone, thou false, deluding slave,

                                                       [*She*] *beats him.*

That feed'st me with the very name of meat!
Sorrow on thee and all the pack of you,
That triumph thus upon my misery!
Go, get thee gone, I say.

Enter Petruchio and Hortensio with meat.

Petruchio
How fares my Kate? What, sweeting, all amort?
Hortensio
Mistress, what cheer?
Katharina   Faith, as cold as can be.
Petruchio
Pluck up thy spirits; look cheerfully upon me.
Here, love, thou seest how diligent I am
To dress thy meat myself and bring it thee.
I am sure, sweet Kate, this kindness merits thanks.
What, not a word? Nay, then thou lov'st it not,
And all my pains is sorted to no proof.
Here, take away this dish.
Katharina   I pray you, let it stand.
Petruchio
The poorest service is repaid with thanks,
And so shall mine before you touch the meat.
Katharina   I thank you, sir.
Hortensio
Signor Petruchio, fie, you are to blame.
Come, Mistress Kate, I'll bear you company.

[*They sit at table.*]

Petruchio [*aside to Hortensio*]
Eat it up all, Hortensio, if thou lovest me.—
Much good do it unto thy gentle heart!
Kate, eat apace. And now, my honey love,
Will we return unto thy father's house
And revel it as bravely as the best,
With silken coats and caps and golden rings,
With ruffs, and cuffs, and farthingales, and things,
With scarves, and fans, and double change of bravery,
With amber bracelets, beads, and all this knavery.
What, hast thou dined? The tailor stays thy leisure,
To deck thy body with his ruffling treasure.

Enter Tailor [with a gown].

Come, tailor, let us see these ornaments.
Lay forth the gown.

Enter Haberdasher [with a cap].

What news with you, sir?

Haberdasher
Here is the cap your worship did bespeak.
Petruchio
Why, this was molded on a porringer—
A velvet dish. Fie, fie, 'tis lewd and filthy.
Why, 'tis a cockle or a walnut shell,
A knack, a toy, a trick, a baby's cap.
Away with it! Come, let me have a bigger.
Katharina
I'll have no bigger. This doth fit the time,
And gentlewomen wear such caps as these.
Petruchio
When you are gentle, you shall have one too,
And not till then.
Hortensio [aside]   That will not be in haste.
Katharina
Why, sir, I trust I may have leave to speak,
And speak I will. I am no child, no babe.
Your betters have endured me say my mind,
And if you cannot, best you stop your ears.
My tongue will tell the anger of my heart,
Or else my heart, concealing it, will break.
And rather than it shall, I will be free
Even to the uttermost, as I please, in words.
Petruchio
Why, thou sayst true. It is a paltry cap,
A custard-coffin, a bauble, a silken pie.
I love thee well in that thou lik'st it not.
Katharina
Love me or love me not, I like the cap,

And it I will have, or I will have none.

                                 [Exit Haberdasher.]

Petruchio

    Thy gown? Why, ay. Come, tailor, let us see 't.
    O, mercy, God, what masquing stuff is here?
    What's this, a sleeve? 'Tis like a demicannon.
    What, up and down carved like an apple tart?
    Here's snip, and nip, and cut, and slish and slash,
    Like to a censer in a barber's shop.
    Why, what i' devil's name, tailor, call'st thou this?

Hortensio *[aside]*

    I see she's like to have neither cap nor gown.

Tailor

    You bid me make it orderly and well,
    According to the fashion and the time.

Petruchio

    Marry, and did. But if you be remembered,
    I did not bid you mar it to the time.

Go hop me over every kennel home,

For you shall hop without my custom, sir.

I'll none of it. Hence, make your best of it.

Katharina

I never saw a better fashioned gown,

More quaint, more pleasing, nor more commendable.

Belike you mean to make a puppet of me.

Petruchio

Why, true, he means to make a puppet of thee.

Tailor

She says your worship means to make a puppet of her.

Petruchio

O, monstrous arrogance! Thou liest, thou thread, thou thimble,

Thou yard, three-quarters, half-yard, quarter, nail!

Thou flea, thou nit, thou winter cricket, thou!

Braved in mine own house with a skein of thread?

Away, thou rag, thou quantity, thou remnant,

Or I shall so be-mete thee with thy yard

As thou shalt think on prating whilst thou liv'st!

I tell thee, I, that thou hast marred her gown.

Tailor

Your worship is deceived. The gown is made

Just as my master had direction.

Grumio gave order how it should be done.

Grumio   I gave him no order. I gave him the stuff.

Tailor

But how did you desire it should be made?

Grumio   Marry, sir, with needle and thread.

Tailor

But did you not request to have it cut?

Grumio   Thou hast faced many things.

Tailor   I have.

Grumio   Face not me. Thou hast braved many men; brave not me. I
will neither be faced nor braved. I say unto thee, I bid thy master
cut out the gown, but I did not bid him cut it to pieces. Ergo, thou
liest.

Tailor   Why, here is the note of the fashion to testify.

[He displays his bill.]

Petruchio   Read it.

Grumio   The note lies in 's throat if he say I said so.

Tailor [*reads*]   "Imprimis, a loose-bodied gown—"

Grumio   Master, if ever I said loose-bodied gown, sew me in the skirts
of it and beat me to death with a bottom of brown thread. I said a
gown.

Petruchio   Proceed.

Tailor [*reads*]   "With a small compassed cape—"

Grumio   I confess the cape.

Tailor [*reads*]   "With a trunk sleeve—"

Grumio   I confess two sleeves.

Tailor [*reads*]   "The sleeves curiously cut."

Petruchio   Ay, there's the villainy.

Grumio   Error i' the bill, sir, error i' the bill. I commanded the sleeves should be cut out and sewed up again, and that I'll prove upon thee, though thy little finger be armed in a thimble.

Tailor   This is true that I say. An I had thee in place where, thou shouldst know it.

Grumio   I am for thee straight. Take thou the bill, give me thy mete-yard, and spare not me.

Hortensio   God-a-mercy, Grumio, then he shall have no odds.

Petruchio   Well, sir, in brief, the gown is not for me.

Grumio   You are i' the right, sir, 'tis for my mistress.

Petruchio   Go, take it up unto thy master's use.

Grumio [*to the Tailor*]   Villain, not for thy life! Take up my mistress' gown for thy master's use!

Petruchio   Why sir, what's your conceit in that?

Grumio

O, sir, the conceit is deeper than you think for:
Take up my mistress' gown to his master's use!
O, fie, fie, fie!

Petruchio [*aside to Hortensio*]

Hortensio, say thou wilt see the tailor paid.
[*To Tailor.*] Go, take it hence. Begone, and say no more.

Hortensio [*aside to the Tailor*]

Tailor, I'll pay thee for thy gown tomorrow.
Take no unkindness of his hasty words.
Away, I say. Commend me to thy master.

[*Exit Tailor.*]

Petruchio

Well, come, my Kate. We will unto your father's
Even in these honest, mean habiliments.
Our purses shall be proud, our garments poor,
For 'tis the mind that makes the body rich;
And as the sun breaks through the darkest clouds,
So honor peereth in the meanest habit,

What, is the jay more precious than the lark
Because his feathers are more beautiful?
Or is the adder better than the eel
Because his painted skin contents the eye?
O, no, good Kate; neither art thou the worse
For this poor furniture and mean array.
If thou account'st it shame, lay it on me.
And therefore frolic; we will hence forthwith,
To feast and sport us at thy father's house.
[*To Grumio.*] Go call my men, and let us straight to him;
And bring our horses unto Long Lane end.
There will we mount, and thither walk on foot.
Let's see, I think 'tis now some seven o'clock,
And well we may come there by dinnertime.

Katharina
I dare assure you, sir, 'tis almost two,
And 'twill be suppertime ere you come there.

Petruchio
It shall be seven ere I go to horse.
Look what I speak, or do, or think to do,
You are still crossing it.— Sirs, let 't alone.
I will not go today, and ere I do,
It shall be what o'clock I say it is.

Hortensio [*aside*]
Why, so this gallant will command the sun.

[*Exeunt*]

4.4 ENTER TRANIO [AS LUCENTIO], AND THE PEDANT
DRESSED LIKE VINCENTIO [BOOTED].

Tranio
Sir, this is the house. Please it you that I call?

Pedant
Ay, what else? And but I be deceived,
Signor Baptista may remember me,
Near twenty years ago, in Genoa—

Tranio
> Where we were lodgers at the Pegasus.—
> 'Tis well; and hold your own in any case
> With such austerity as 'longeth to a father.

> *Enter Biondello.*

Pedant
> I warrant you. But, sir, here comes your boy.
> 'Twere good he were schooled.

Tranio
> Fear you not him.— Sirrah Biondello,
> Now do your duty throughly, I advise you.
> Imagine 'twere the right Vincentio.

Biondello   Tut, fear not me.

Tranio
> But hast thou done thy errand to Baptista?

Biondello
> I told him mat your father was at Venice
> And that you looked for him this day in Padua.

Tranio *[giving money]*
> Thou'rt a tall fellow. Hold thee that to drink.
> Here comes Baptista. Set your countenance, sir.

> *Enter Baptista, and Lucentio [as Cambio].*
> *[The] Pedant [stands] bareheaded.*

> Signor Baptista, you are happily met.
> [*To the Pedant.*] Sir, this is the gentleman I told you of.
> I pray you, stand good father to me now;
> Give me Bianca for my patrimony.

Pedant   Soft, son!—
> Sir, by your leave, having come to Padua
> To gather in some debts, my son Lucentio
> Made me acquainted with a weighty cause
> Of love between your daughter and himself;
> And, for the good report I hear of you
> And for the love he beareth to your daughter

And she to him, to stay him not too long,
I am content, in a good father's care,
To have him matched. And if you please to like
No worse than I, upon some agreement
Me shall you find ready and willing
With one consent to have her so bestowed;
For curious I cannot be with you,
Signor Baptista, of whom I hear so well.

Baptista

Sir, pardon me in what I have to say.
Your plainness and your shortness please me well.
Right true it is your son Lucentio here
Doth love my daughter, and she loveth him,
Or both dissemble deeply their affections.
And therefore, if you say no more than this,
That like a father you will deal with him
And pass my daughter a sufficient dower,
The match is made, and all is done.
Your son shall have my daughter with consent.

Tranio

I thank you, sir. Where then do you know best
We be affied and such assurance ta'en
As shall with either part's agreement stand?

Baptista

Not in my house, Lucentio, for you know
Pitchers have ears, and I have many servants.
Besides, old Gremio is hearkening still,
And happily we might be interrupted.

Tranio

Then at my lodging, an it like you.
There doth my father lie, and there this night
We'll pass the business privately and well.
Send for your daughter by your servant here.

                    [*He indicates Lucentio, and winks at him.*]

My boy shall fetch the scrivener presently.

The worst is this, that at so slender warning
You are like to have a thin and slender pittance.

Baptista
It likes me well. Cambio, hie you home,
And bid Bianca make her ready straight.
And if you will, tell what hath happened:
Lucentio's father is arrived in Padua,
And how she's like to be Lucentio's wife.

[Exit Lucentio.]

Biondello
I pray the gods she may with all my heart!
Tranio
Dally not with the gods, but get thee gone.

Exit [Biondello].

Signor Baptista, shall I lead the way?
Welcome! One mess is like to be your cheer.
Come, sir, we will better it in Pisa.

Baptista   I follow you.

Exeunt [Tranio, Pedant, and Baptista].

Enter Lucentio [as Cambio] and Biondello.

Biondello   Cambio!
Lucentio   What sayst thou, Biondello?
Biondello   You saw my master wink and laugh upon you?
Lucentio   Biondello, what of that?
Biondello   Faith, nothing; but he's left me here behind to expound the meaning or moral of his signs and tokens.
Lucentio   I pray thee, moralize them.
Biondello   Then thus. Baptista is safe, talking with the deceiving father of a deceitful son.
Lucentio   And what of him?
Biondello   His daughter is to be brought by you to the supper.
Lucentio   And then?
Biondello   The old priest at Saint Luke's church is at your command at all hours.

Lucentio   And what of all this?

Biondello   I cannot tell, except they are busied about a counterfeit assurance. Take you assurance of her *cum privilegio ad imprimendum solum*. To the church take the priest, clerk, and some sufficient honest witnesses.

If this be not that you look for, I have no more to say,
But bid Bianca farewell forever and a day.

[*Biondello starts to leave.*]

Lucentio   Hear'st thou, Biondello?

Biondello   I cannot tarry. I knew a wench married in an afternoon as she went to the garden for parsley to stuff a rabbit, and so may you, sir. And so, adieu, sir. My master hath appointed me to go to Saint Luke's, to bid the priest be ready to come against you come with your appendix.   [*Exit.*]

Lucentio

I may, and will, if she be so contented.
She will be pleased; then wherefore should I doubt?
Hap what hap may, I'll roundly go about her.
It shall go hard if Cambio go without her.   [*Exit.*]

4.5 ENTER PETRUCHIO, KATE, [AND] HORTENSIO.

Petruchio

Come on, i' God's name, once more toward our father's.
Good Lord, how bright and goodly shines the moon!

Katharina

The moon? The sun. It is not moonlight now.

Petruchio

I say it is the moon that shines so bright.

Katharina

I know it is the sun that shines so bright

Petruchio

Now, by my mother's son, and that's myself,
It shall be moon, or star, or what I list
Or ere I journey to your father's house.—

Go on, and fetch our horses back again—
Evermore crossed and crossed, nothing but crossed!

Hortensio [*to Katharina*]

Say as he says, or we shall never go.

Katharina

Forward, I pray, since we have come so far,
And be it moon, or sun, or what you please;
An if you please to call it a rush candle,
Henceforth I vow it shall be so for me.

Petruchio

I say it is the moon.

Katharina   I know it is the moon.

Petruchio

Nay, then you lie. It is the blessèd sun.

Katharina

Then, God be blessed, it is the blessèd sun.
But sun it is not, when you say it is not,
And the moon changes even as your mind.
What you will have it named, even that it is,
And so it shall be so for Katharine.

Hortensio

Petruchio, go thy ways. The field is won.

Petruchio

Well, forward, forward. Thus the bowl should run,
And not unluckily against the bias.
But soft! Company is coming here.

Enter Vincentio.

[*To Vincentio.*] Good morrow, gentle mistress. Where away?—
Tell me, sweet Kate, and tell me truly too,
Hast thou beheld a fresher gentlewoman?
Such war of white and red within her cheeks!
What stars do spangle heaven with such beauty
As those two eyes become that heavenly face?—
Fair lovely maid, once more good day to thee.—

Sweet Kate, embrace her for her beauty's sake.
Hortensio [*aside*]
    'A will make the man mad, to make a woman of him.
Katharina [*embracing Vincentio*]
    Young budding virgin, fair, and fresh, and sweet,
    Whither away, or where is thy abode?
    Happy the parents of so fair a child!
    Happier the man whom favorable stars
    Allots thee for his lovely bedfellow!
Petruchio
    Why, how now, Kate? I hope thou art not mad.
    This is a man, old, wrinkled, faded, withered,
    And not a maiden, as thou sayst he is.
Katharina
    Pardon, old father, my mistaking eyes,
    That have been so bedazzled with the sun
    That everything I look on seemeth green.
    Now I perceive thou art a reverend father.
    Pardon, I pray thee, for my mad mistaking.
Petruchio
    Do, good old grandsire, and withal make known
    Which way thou travelest—if along with us,
    We shall be joyful of thy company.
Vincentio
    Fair sir, and you, my merry mistress,
    That with your strange encounter much amazed me,
    My name is called Vincentio, my dwelling Pisa,
    And bound I am to Padua, there to visit
    A son of mine, which long I have not seen.
Petruchio
    What is his name?
Vincentio   Lucentio, gentle sir.
Petruchio
    Happily met, the happier for thy son.
    And now by law as well as reverend age
    I may entitle thee my loving father.

The sister to my wife, this gentlewoman,
Thy son by this hath married. Wonder not,
Nor be not grieved. She is of good esteem,
Her dowry wealthy, and of worthy birth;
Besides, so qualified as may beseem
The spouse of any noble gentleman.
Let me embrace with old Vincentio,
And wander we to see thy honest son,
Who will of thy arrival be full joyous.

[He embraces Vincentio.]

Vincentio
But is this true? Or is it else your pleasure,
Like pleasant travelers, to break a jest
Upon the company you overtake?
Hortensio
I do assure thee, father, so it is.
Petruchio
Come, go along, and see the truth hereof,
For our first merriment hath made thee jealous.

Exeunt [all but Hortensio].

Hortensio
Well, Petruchio, this has put me in heart.
Have to my widow! And if she be froward,
Then hast thou taught Hortensio to be untoward.   *[Exit.]*

*5.1 ENTER BIONDELLO, LUCENTIO [NO LONGER DISGUISED], AND
BIANCA. GREMIO IS OUT BEFORE [AND STANDS ASIDE].*

Biondello   Softly and swiftly, sir, for the priest is ready.
Lucentio   I fly, Biondello. But they may chance to need thee at home;
therefore leave us.
Biondello   Nay, faith, I'll see the church a' your back, and then come
back to my master's as soon as I can.

[Exeunt Lucentio, Bianca, and Biondello.]

Gremio
I marvel Cambio comes not all this while.

Enter Petruchio, Kate, Vincentio, Grumio, with attendants.

Petruchio

Sir, here's the door. This is Lucentio's house.

My father's bears more toward the marketplace;

Thither must I, and here I leave you, sir.

Vincentio

You shall not choose but drink before you go.

I think I shall command your welcome here,

And by all likelihood some cheer is toward.   [*Knock.*]

Gremio [*advancing*]   They're busy within. You were best knock louder.

[*Pedant looks out of the window.*]

Pedant   What's he that knocks as he would beat down the gate?

Vincentio   Is Signor Lucentio within, sir?

Pedant   He's within, sir, but not to be spoken withal.

Vincentio   What if a man bring him a hundred pound or two to make merry withal?

Pedant   Keep your hundred pounds to yourself. He shall need none, so long as I live.

Petruchio [*to Vincentio*]   Nay, I told you your son was well beloved in Padua.—Do you hear, sir? To leave frivolous circumstances, I pray you, tell Signor Lucentio that his father is come from Pisa and is here at the door to speak with him.

Pedant   Thou liest. His father is come from Padua and here looking out at the window.

Vincentio   Art thou his father?

Pedant   Ay, sir, so his mother says, if I may believe her.

Petruchio [*to Vincentio*]   Why, how now, gentleman! Why, this is flat knavery, to take upon you another man's name.

Pedant   Lay hands on the villain. I believe 'a means to cozen somebody in this city under my countenance.

Enter Biondello.

Biondello [*aside*]   I have seen them in the church together, God send 'em good shipping! But who is here? Mine old master Vincentio! Now we are undone and brought to nothing.

Vincentio [*seeing Biondello*]   Come hither, crackhemp.

Biondello   I hope I may choose, sir.

Vincentio   Come hither, you rogue. What, have you forgot me?

Biondello   Forgot you? No, sir. I could not forget you, for I never saw you before in all my life.

Vincentio   What, you notorious villain, didst thou never see thy master's father, Vincentio?

Biondello   What, my old worshipful old master? Yes, marry, sir, see where he looks out of the window.

Vincentio   Is 't so, indeed?   [*He beats Biondello.*]

Biondello   Help, help, help! Here's a madman will murder me. [*Exit.*]

Pedant   Help, son! Help, Signor Baptista!

[*Exit from the window.*]

Petruchio   Prithee, Kate, let's stand aside and see the end of this controversy.   [*They stand aside.*]

Enter [below] Pedant with servants, Baptista,
[and] Tranio [as Lucentio].

Tranio   Sir, what are you that offer to beat my servant?

Vincentio   What am I, sir? Nay, what are you, sir? O immortal gods!
O fine villain! A silken doublet, a velvet hose, a scarlet cloak, and
a copintank hat! O, I am undone, I am undone! While I play the
good husband at home, my son and my servant spend all at the
university.

Tranio   How now, what's the matter?

Baptista   What, is the man lunatic?

Tranio   Sir, you seem a sober ancient gentleman by your habit, but
your words show you a madman. Why, sir, what 'cerns it you if I
wear pearl and gold? I thank my good father, I am able to maintain
it.

Vincentio   Thy father! O villain, he is a sailmaker in Bergamo.

Baptista   You mistake, sir, you mistake, sir. Pray, what do you think
is his name?

Vincentio   His name! As if I knew not his name! I have brought him up ever since he was three years old, and his name is Tranio.

Pedant   Away, away, mad ass! His name is Lucentio, and he is mine only son, and heir to the lands of me, Signor Vincentio.

Vincentio   Lucentio! O, he hath murdered his master! Lay hold on him, I charge you, in the Duke's name. O, my son, my son! Tell me, thou villain, where is my son Lucentio?

Tranio   Call forth an officer.

[Enter an Officer.]

Carry this mad knave to the jail. Father Baptista, I charge you see that he be forthcoming.

Vincentio   Carry me to the jail?

Gremio   Stay, officer, he shall not go to prison.

Baptista   Talk not, Signor Gremio. I say he shall go to prison.

Gremio   Take heed, Signor Baptista, lest you be coney-catched in this business. I dare swear this is the right Vincentio.

Pedant   Swear, if thou dar'st.

Gremio   Nay, I dare not swear it.

Tranio   Then thou wert best say that I am not Lucentio.

Gremio   Yes, I know thee to be Signor Lucentio.

Baptista   Away with the dotard! To the jail with him!

Enter Biondello, Lucentio, and Bianca.

Vincentio   Thus strangers may be haled and abused—O monstrous villain!

Biondello   O! We are spoiled and—yonder he is. Deny him, forswear him, or else we are all undone.

Exeunt Biondello, Tranio, and Pedant, as fast as may be.
[Lucentio and Bianca] kneel.

Lucentio
   Pardon, sweet Father.

Vincentio   Lives my sweet son?

Bianca
   Pardon, dear Father.

Baptista   How hast thou offended?

Where is Lucentio?

Lucentio   Here's Lucentio,
    Right son to the right Vincentio,
    That have by marriage made thy daughter mine,
    While counterfeit supposes bleared thine eyne.

Gremio
    Here's packing, with a witness, to deceive us all!

Vincentio
    Where is that damnèd villain Tranio,
    That faced and braved me in this matter so?

Baptista
    Why, tell me, is not this my Cambio?

Bianca
    Cambio is changed into Lucentio.

Lucentio
    Love wrought these miracles. Bianca's love
    Made me exchange my state with Tranio,
    While he did bear my countenance in the town,
    And happily I have arrivèd at the last
    Unto the wishèd haven of my bliss.
    What Tranio did, myself enforced him to;
    Then pardon him, sweet Father, for my sake.

Vincentio   I'll slit the villain's nose, that would have sent me to the jail.

Baptista [*to Lucentio*]   But do you hear, sir? Have you married my daughter without asking my good will?

Vincentio   Fear not, Baptista, we will content you. Go to. But I will in, to be revenged for the villainy.

                                          [*Exit.*]

Baptista   And I, to sound the depth of this knavery.

                                          [*Exit.*]

Lucentio   Look not pale, Bianca. Thy father will not frown.

                         Exeunt [*Lucentio and Bianca*].

Gremio
    My cake is dough, but I'll in among the rest,
    Out of hope of all but my share of the feast.   [*Exit.*]

Katharina   Husband, let's follow, to see the end of this ado.
Petruchio   First kiss me, Kate, and we will.
Katharina   What, in the midst of the street?
Petruchio   What, art thou ashamed of me?
Katharina   No, sir, God forbid, but ashamed to kiss.
Petruchio

    Why, then let's home again. [*To Grumio.*] Come, sirrah, let's away.
Katharina

    Nay, I will give thee a kiss. [*She kisses him.*] Now pray thee, love, stay.
Petruchio

    Is not this well? Come, my sweet Kate.
    Better once than never, for never too late.   [*Exeunt.*]

5.2 ENTER BAPTISTA, VINCENTIO, GREMIO, THE PEDANT,
LUCENTIO, AND BIANCA; [PETRUCHIO, KATE, HORTENSIO,]
TRANIO, BIONDELLO, GRUMIO, AND [THE] WIDOW;
THE SERVINGMEN WITH TRANIO BRINGING IN A BANQUET.

Lucentio

    At last, though long, our jarring notes agree,
    And time it is, when raging war is done,
    To smile at scapes and perils overblown.
    My fair Bianca, bid my father welcome,
    While I with selfsame kindness welcome thine.
    Brother Petruchio, sister Katharina,
    And thou, Hortensio, with thy loving widow,
    Feast with the best, and welcome to my house.
    My banquet is to close our stomachs up
    After our great good cheer. Pray you, sit down,
    For now we sit to chat as well as eat.   [*They sit.*]
Petruchio

    Nothing but sit and sit, and eat and eat!
Baptista

    Padua affords this kindness, son Petruchio.
Petruchio

    Padua affords nothing but what is kind.

Hortensio

For both our sakes, I would that word were true.

Petruchio

Now, for my life, Hortensio fears his widow.

Widow

Then never trust me if I be afeard.

Petruchio

You are very sensible, and yet you miss my sense:
I mean Hortensio is afeard of you.

Widow

He that is giddy thinks the world turns round.

Petruchio

Roundly replied.

Katharina   Mistress, how mean you that?

Widow   Thus I conceive by him.

Petruchio

Conceives by me! How likes Hortensio that?

Hortensio

My widow says, thus she conceives her tale.

Petruchio

Very well mended. Kiss him for that, good widow.

Katharina

"He that is giddy thinks the world turns round":
I pray you, tell me what you meant by that.

Widow

Your husband, being troubled with a shrew,
Measures my husband's sorrow by his woe.
And now you know my meaning.

Katharina

A very mean meaning.

Widow   Right, I mean you.

Katharina

And I am mean indeed, respecting you.

Petruchio   To her, Kate!

Hortensio   To her, widow!

Petruchio
    A hundred marks, my Kate does put her down.
Hortensio   That's my office.
Petruchio
    Spoke like an officer. Ha' to thee, lad!

                                            [He] *drinks to Hortensio.*

Baptista
    How likes Gremio these quick-witted folks?
Gremio
    Believe me, sir, they butt together well.
Bianca
    Head, and butt! An hasty-witted body
    Would say your head and butt were head and horn.
Vincentio
    Ay, mistress bride, hath that awakened you?
Bianca
    Ay, but not frighted me. Therefore I'll sleep again.

Petruchio

Nay, that you shall not. Since you have begun,
Have at you for a bitter jest or two!

Bianca

Am I your bird? I mean to shift my bush;
And then pursue me as you draw your bow.
You are welcome all.

                    Exit Bianca [with Katharina and the Widow].

Petruchio

She hath prevented me. Here, Signor Tranio,
This bird you aimed at, though you hit her not.
Therefore a health to all that shot and missed.

                              [He offers a toast.]

Tranio

O, sir, Lucentio slipped me like his greyhound,
Which runs himself and catches for his master.

Petruchio

A good swift simile, but something currish.

Tranio

'Tis well, sir, that you hunted for yourself.
'Tis thought your deer does hold you at a bay.

Baptista

O ho, Petruchio! Tranio hits you now.

Lucentio

I thank thee for that gird, good Tranio.

Hortensio

Confess, confess, hath he not hit you here?

Petruchio

'A has a little galled me, I confess;
And as the jest did glance away from me,
'Tis ten to one it maimed you two outright.

Baptista

Now, in good sadness, son Petruchio,
I think thou hast the veriest shrew of all.

Petruchio

Well, I say no. And therefore for assurance

Let's each one send unto his wife;
And he whose wife is most obedient
To come at first when he doth send for her
Shall win the wager which we will propose.
Hortensio
Content. What's the wager?
Lucentio   Twenty crowns.
Petruchio   Twenty crowns!
   I'll venture so much of my hawk or hound,
   But twenty times so much upon my wife.
Lucentio   A hundred then.
Hortensio   Content.
Petruchio   A match. 'Tis done.
Hortensio   Who shall begin?
Lucentio   That will I.
   Go, Biondello, bid your mistress come to me.
Biondello   I go.   [*Exit.*]
Baptista
   Son, I'll be your half Bianca comes.
Lucentio
   I'll have no halves; I'll bear it all myself.

Enter Biondello.

   How now, what news?
Biondello
   Sir, my mistress sends you word
   That she is busy and she cannot come.
Petruchio
   How? She's busy and she cannot come?
   Is that an answer?
Gremio   Ay, and a kind one too.
   Pray God, sir, your wife send you not a worse.
Petruchio   I hope better.
Hortensio
   Sirrah Biondello, go and entreat my wife
   To come to me forthwith.   [*Exit Biondello.*]

Petruchio   Oho, entreat her!
  Nay, then she must needs come.
Hortensio   I am afraid, sir,
  Do what you can, yours will not be entreated.

                    Enter Biondello.

  Now, where's my wife?
Biondello
  She says you have some goodly jest in hand.
  She will not come. She bids you come to her.
Petruchio
  Worse and worse. She will not come!
  O, vile, intolerable, not to be endured!
  Sirrah Grumio, go to your mistress.
  Say I command her come to me.   *Exit [Grumio].*
Hortensio
  I know her answer.
Petruchio   What?
Hortensio   She will not.
Petruchio
  The fouler fortune mine, and there an end.

                    Enter Katharina.

Baptista
  Now, by my halidom, here comes Katharina!
Katharina
  What is your will, sir, that you send for me?
Petruchio
  Where is your sister, and Hortensio's wife?
Katharina
  They sit conferring by the parlor fire.
Petruchio
  Go fetch them hither. If they deny to come,
  Swinge me them soundly forth unto their husbands.
  Away, I say, and bring them hither straight.

                                        [Exit Katharina.]

Lucentio

Here is a wonder, if you talk of a wonder.

Hortensio

And so it is. I wonder what it bodes.

Petruchio

Marry, peace it bodes, and love, and quiet life,

An awful rule, and right supremacy,

And, to be short, what not that's sweet and happy.

Baptista

Now, fair befall thee, good Petruchio!

The wager thou hast won, and I will add

Unto their losses twenty thousand crowns,

Another dowry to another daughter,

For she is changed, as she had never been.

Petruchio

Nay, I will win my wager better yet,

And show more sign of her obedience,

Her new-built virtue and obedience.

Enter Kate, Bianca, and [the] Widow.

See where she comes and brings your froward wives

As prisoners to her womanly persuasion.—

Katharine, that cap of yours becomes you not.

Off with that bauble. Throw it underfoot.

[*She obeys.*]

Widow

Lord, let me never have a cause to sigh

Till I be brought to such a silly pass!

Bianca

Fie, what a foolish duty call you this?

Lucentio

I would your duty were as foolish, too.

The wisdom of your duty, fair Bianca,

Hath cost me a hundred crowns since suppertime.

Bianca

The more fool you, for laying on my duty.

Petruchio

    Katharine, I charge thee tell these headstrong women

    What duty they do owe their lords and husbands.

Widow

    Come, come, you're mocking. We will have no telling.

Petruchio

    Come on, I say, and first begin with her.

Widow   She shall not.

Petruchio

    I say she shall—and first begin with her.

Katharina

    Fie, fie! Unknit that threatening, unkind brow,

    And dart not scornful glances from those eyes

    To wound thy lord, thy king, thy governor.

    It blots thy beauty as frosts do bite the meads,

    Confounds thy fame as whirlwinds shake fair buds,

    And in no sense is meet or amiable.

A woman moved is like a fountain troubled,
Muddy, ill-seeming, thick, bereft of beauty;
And while it is so, none so dry or thirsty
Will deign to sip or touch one drop of it.
Thy husband is thy lord, thy life, thy keeper,
Thy head, thy sovereign; one that cares for thee,
And for thy maintenance commits his body
To painful labor both by sea and land,
To watch the night in storms, the day in cold,
Whilst thou liest warm at home, secure and safe;
And craves no other tribute at thy hands
But love, fair looks, and true obedience—
Too little payment for so great a debt.
Such duty as the subject owes the prince,
Even such a woman oweth to her husband;
And when she is froward, peevish, sullen, sour,
And not obedient to his honest will,
What is she but a foul contending rebel
And graceless traitor to her loving lord?
I am ashamed that women are so simple
To offer war where they should kneel for peace,
Or seek for rule, supremacy, and sway,
When they are bound to serve, love, and obey.
Why are our bodies soft, and weak, and smooth,
Unapt to toil and trouble in the world,
But that our soft conditions and our hearts
Should well agree with our external parts?
Come, come, you froward and unable worms!
My mind hath been as big as one of yours,
My heart as great, my reason haply more,
To bandy word for word and frown for frown;
But now I see our lances are but straws,
Our strength as weak, our weakness past compare,
That seeming to be most which we indeed least are.
Then vail your stomachs, for it is no boot,
And place your hands below your husband's foot,

In token of which duty, if he please,
My hand is ready; may it do him ease.

Petruchio

Why, there's a wench! Come on, and kiss me, Kate.

[*They kiss.*]

Lucentio

Well, go thy ways, old lad, for thou shalt ha 't.

Vincentio

'Tis a good hearing when children are toward.

Lucentio

But a harsh hearing when women are froward.

Petruchio   Come, Kate, we'll to bed.

We three are married, but you two are sped.

[*To Lucentio.*] 'Twas I won the wager, though you hit the white,
And, being a winner, God give you good night!

Exit Petruchio [and Katharina].

Hortensio

Now go thy ways. Thou hast tamed a curst shrew.

Lucentio

'Tis a wonder, by your leave, she will be tamed so.

[*Exeunt.*]

As You Like It

As You Like It

DRAMATIS PERSONAE

Duke Senior, a banished duke
Duke Frederick, his usurping brother
Rosalind, daughter of Duke Senior, later disguised as
    Ganymede
Celia, daughter of Duke Frederick, later disguised as
    Aliena
Oliver, Jaques, Orlando, sons of Sir Rowland de Boys
Amiens, Jaques, lords attending Duke Senior
Le Beau, a courtier attending Duke Frederick
Charles, a wrestler in the court of Duke Frederick
Adam, an aged servant of Oliver and then Orlando
Dennis, a servant of Oliver
Touchstone, the *clown*
Corin, an old shepherd
Silvius, a young shepherd, in love with Phoebe
Phoebe, a shepherdess
William, a country youth, in love with Audrey
Audrey, a country wench
Sir Oliver Mar-text, a country vicar
Hymen, god of marriage
Lords and Attendants waiting on Duke Frederick
    and Duke Senior

Scene: Oliver's house; Duke Frederick's court; and
the Forest of Arden

1.1 ENTER ORLANDO AND ADAM.

Orlando   As I remember, Adam, it was upon this fashion bequeathed me by will but poor a thousand crowns and, as thou sayst, charged my brother on his blessing to breed me well; and there begins my sadness. My brother Jaques he keeps at school, and report speaks goldenly of his profit. For my part, he keeps me rustically at home— or, to speak more properly, stays me here at home unkept; for call you that "keeping" for a gentleman of my birth, that differs not from the stalling of an ox? His horses are bred better, for besides that they are fair with their feeding, they are taught their manage, and to that end riders dearly hired. But I, his brother, gain nothing under him but growth, for the which his animals on his dunghills are as much bound to him as I. Besides this nothing that he so plentifully gives me, the something that nature gave me his counte- nance seems to take from me. He lets me feed with his hinds, bars me the place of a brother, and as much as in him lies, mines my gentility with my education. This is it, Adam, that grieves me; and the spirit of my father, which I think is within me, begins to mutiny against this servitude. I will no longer endure it, though yet I know no wise remedy how to avoid it.

Enter Oliver.

Adam   Yonder comes my master, your brother.

Orlando   Go apart, Adam, and thou shalt hear how he will shake me up.   [*Adam stands aside.*]

Oliver   Now, sir, what make you here?

Orlando   Nothing. I am not taught to make anything.

Oliver   What mar you then, sir?

Orlando   Marry, sir, I am helping you to mar that which God made, a poor unworthy brother of yours, with idleness.

Oliver   Marry, sir, be better employed, and be naught awhile.

Orlando   Shall I keep your hogs and eat husks with them? What prod- igal portion have I spent, that I should come to such penury?

Oliver   Know you where you are, sir?

Orlando   O, sir, very well: here in your orchard.

Oliver   Know you before whom, sir?

Orlando   Ay, better than him I am before knows me. I know you are my eldest brother, and in the gentle condition of blood you should so know me. The courtesy of nations allows you my better, in that you are the firstborn, but the same tradition takes not away my blood, were there twenty brothers betwixt us. I have as much of my father in me as you, albeit I confess your coming before me is nearer to his reverence.

Oliver   What, boy!   [*He strikes Orlando.*]

Orlando   Come, come, elder brother, you are too young in this.

[*He seizes Oliver by the throat.*]

Oliver   Wilt thou lay hands on me, villain?

Orlando   I am no villain. I am the youngest son of Sir Rowland de Boys. He was my father, and he is thrice a villain that says such a father begot villains. Wert thou not my brother, I would not take this hand from thy throat till this other had pulled out thy tongue for saying so. Thou hast railed on thyself.

Adam   Sweet masters, be patient! For your father's remembrance, be at accord.

Oliver   Let me go, I say.

Orlando   I will not till I please. You shall hear me. My father charged you in his will to give me good education. You have trained me like a peasant, obscuring and hiding from me all gentlemanlike qualities. The spirit of my father grows strong in me, and I will no longer endure it; therefore allow me such exercises as may become a gentleman, or give me the poor allottery my father left me by testament. With that I will go buy my fortunes.   [*He releases Oliver.*]

Oliver   And what wilt thou do? Beg when that is spent? Well, sir, get you in. I will not long be troubled with you; you shall have some part of your will. I pray you, leave me.

Orlando   I will no further offend you than becomes me for my good.

Oliver [*to Adam*]   Get you with him, you old dog.

Adam   Is "old dog" my reward? Most true, I have lost my teeth in your service. God be with my old master! He would not have spoke such a word.

Exeunt Orlando [*and*] *Adam.*

Oliver   Is it even so? Begin you to grow upon me? I will physic your rankness and yet give no thousand crowns neither.—Holla, Dennis!

Enter Dennis.

Dennis   Calls your worship?

Oliver   Was not Charles, the Duke's wrestler, here to speak with me?

Dennis   So please you, he is here at the door and importunes access to you.

Oliver   Call him in. [*Exit Dennis.*] 'Twill be a good way; and tomorrow the wrestling is.

Enter Charles.

Charles   Good morrow to your worship.

Oliver   Good Monsieur Charles, what's the new news at the new court?

Charles   There's no news at the court, sir, but the old news: that is, the old Duke is banished by his younger brother the new Duke, and three or four loving lords have put themselves into voluntary exile with him, whose lands and revenues enrich the new Duke; therefore he gives them good leave to wander.

Oliver   Can you tell if Rosalind, the Duke's daughter, be banished with her father?

Charles   O, no; for the Duke's daughter, her cousin, so loves her, being ever from their cradles bred together, that she would have followed her exile or have died to stay behind her. She is at the court and no less beloved of her uncle than his own daughter, and never two ladies loved as they do.

Oliver   Where will the old Duke live?

Charles   They say he is already in the Forest of Arden, and a many merry men with him; and there they live like the old Robin Hood of England. They say many young gentlemen flock to him every day and fleet the time carelessly as they did in the golden world.

Oliver   What, you wrestle tomorrow before the new Duke?

Charles   Marry, do I, sir; and I came to acquaint you with a matter. I am given, sir, secretly to understand that your younger brother Orlando hath a disposition to come in disguised against me to try a fall. Tomorrow, sir, I wrestle for my credit, and he that escapes me without some broken limb shall acquit him well. Your brother is but young and tender, and for your love I would be loath to foil him, as I must for my own honor if he come in. Therefore, out of my love to you, I came hither to acquaint you withal, that either you might stay him from his intendment or brook such disgrace well as he shall run into, in that it is a thing of his own search and altogether against my will.

Oliver   Charles, I thank thee for thy love to me, which thou shalt find I will most kindly requite. I had myself notice of my brother's purpose herein and have by underhand means labored to dissuade him from it, but he is resolute. I'll tell thee, Charles, it is the stubbornest young fellow of France, full of ambition, an envious emulator of every man's good parts, a secret and villainous contriver against me his natural brother. Therefore use thy discretion. I had as lief thou didst break his neck as his finger. And thou wert best look to 't; for if thou dost him any slight disgrace, or if he do not mightily grace himself on thee, he will practice against thee by poison, entrap thee by some treacherous device, and never leave thee till he hath ta'en thy life by some indirect means or other; for I assure thee, and almost with tears I speak it, there is not one so young and so villainous this day living. I speak but brotherly of him, but should I anatomize him to thee as he is, I must blush and weep, and thou must look pale and wonder.

Charles   I am heartily glad I came hither to you. If he come tomorrow, I'll give him his payment. If ever he go alone again, I'll never wrestle for prize more. And so God keep your worship!

Oliver   Farewell, good Charles. *Exit [Charles]*. Now will I stir this gamester. I hope I shall see an end of him; for my soul, yet I know not why, hates nothing more than he. Yet he's gentle, never schooled and yet learned, full of noble device, of all sorts enchantingly beloved, and indeed so much in the heart of the world and especially of my own people, who best know him, that I am altogether misprized. But it shall not be so long; this wrestler shall clear all. Nothing remains but that I kindle the boy thither, which now I'll go about.

[*Exit.*]

1.2 ENTER ROSALIND AND CELIA.

Celia   I pray thee, Rosalind, sweet my coz, be merry.

Rosalind   Dear Celia, I show more mirth than I am mistress of, and would you yet I were merrier? Unless you could teach me to forget a banished father, you must not learn me how to remember any extraordinary pleasure.

Celia   Herein I see thou lov'st me not with the full weight that I love thee. If my uncle, thy banished father, had banished thy uncle, the Duke my father, so thou hadst been still with me, I could have taught my love to take thy father for mine. So wouldst thou, if the truth of thy love to me were so righteously tempered as mine is to thee.

Rosalind   Well, I will forget the condition of my estate to rejoice in yours.

Celia   You know my father hath no child but I, nor none is like to have. And truly, when he dies thou shalt be his heir, for what he hath taken away from thy father perforce I will render thee again in affection. By mine honor, I will, and when I break that oath, let me turn monster. Therefore, my sweet Rose, my dear Rose, be merry.

Rosalind   From henceforth I will, coz, and devise sports. Let me see, what think you of falling in love?

Celia   Marry, I prithee, do, to make sport withal. But love no man in good earnest, nor no further in sport neither than with safety of a pure blush thou mayst in honor come off again.

Rosalind   What shall be our sport, then?

Celia   Let us sit and mock the good huswife Fortune from her wheel, that her gifts may henceforth be bestowed equally.

Rosalind   I would we could do so, for her benefits are mightily misplaced, and the bountiful blind woman doth most mistake in her gifts to women.

Celia   'Tis true, for those that she makes fair she scarce makes honest, and those that she makes honest she makes very ill-favoredly.

Rosalind   Nay, now thou goest from Fortune's office to Nature's. Fortune reigns in gifts of the world, not in the lineaments of Nature.

Enter [Touchstone the] Clown.

Celia   No; when Nature hath made a fair creature, may she not by Fortune fall into the fire? Though Nature hath given us wit to flout at Fortune, hath not Fortune sent in this fool to cut off the argument?

Rosalind   Indeed, there is Fortune too hard for Nature, when Fortune makes Nature's natural the cutter-off of Nature's wit.

Celia   Peradventure this is not Fortune's work neither but Nature's, who perceiveth our natural wits too dull to reason of such goddesses and hath sent this natural for our whetstone; for always the dullness of the fool is the whetstone of the wits.—How now, wit, whither wander you?

Touchstone   Mistress, you must come away to your father.

Celia   Were you made the messenger?

Touchstone   No, by mine honor, but I was bid to come for you.

Rosalind   Where learned you that oath, Fool?

Touchstone   Of a certain knight that swore by his honor they were good pancakes and swore by his honor the mustard was naught. Now I'll stand to it the pancakes were naught and the mustard was good, and yet was not the knight forsworn.

Celia   How prove you that in the great heap of your knowledge?

Rosalind   Ay, marry, now unmuzzle your wisdom.

Touchstone   Stand you both forth now. Stroke your chins, and swear by your beards that I am a knave.

Celia   By our beards, if we had them, thou art.

Touchstone   By my knavery, if I had it, then I were; but if you swear by that that is not, you are not forsworn. No more was this knight, swearing by his honor, for he never had any; or if he had, he had sworn it away before ever he saw those pancakes or that mustard.

Celia   Prithee, who is 't that thou mean'st?

Touchstone   One that old Frederick, your father, loves.

Celia   My father's love is enough to honor him enough. Speak no more of him; you'll be whipped for taxation one of these days.

Touchstone   The more pity that fools may not speak wisely what wise men do foolishly.

Celia   By my troth, thou sayest true; for since the little wit that fools have was silenced, the little foolery that wise men have makes a great show. Here comes Monsieur Le Beau.

Enter Le Beau.

Rosalind   With his mouth full of news.

Celia   Which he will put on us as pigeons feed their young.

Rosalind   Then shall we be news-crammed.

Celia   All the better; we shall be the more marketable.—*Bonjour,* Monsieur Le Beau. What's the news?

Le Beau   Fair princess, you have lost much good sport.

Celia   Sport? Of what color?

Le Beau   What color, madam? How shall I answer you?

Rosalind   As wit and fortune will.

Touchstone   Or as the Destinies decrees.

Celia   Well said. That was laid on with a trowel.

Touchstone   Nay, if I keep not my rank—

Rosalind   Thou losest thy old smell.

Le Beau   You amaze me, ladies. I would have told you of good wrestling, which you have lost the sight of.

Rosalind   Yet tell us the manner of the wrestling.

Le Beau   I will tell you the beginning, and if it please your ladyships you may see the end, for the best is yet to do, and here, where you are, they are coming to perform it.

Celia   Well, the beginning, that is dead and buried.

Le Beau   There comes an old man and his three sons—

Celia   I could match this beginning with an old tale.

Le Beau   Three proper young men, of excellent growth and presence—

Rosalind   With bills on their necks, "Be it known unto all men by these presents."

Le Beau   The eldest of the three wrestled with Charles, the Duke's wrestler, which Charles in a moment threw him and broke three of his ribs, that there is little hope of life in him. So he served the second, and so the third. Yonder they lie, the poor old man their father making such pitiful dole over them that all the beholders take his part with weeping.

Rosalind   Alas!

Touchstone   But what is the sport, monsieur, that the ladies have lost?

Le Beau   Why, this that I speak of.

Touchstone   Thus men may grow wiser every day. It is the first time that ever I heard breaking of ribs was sport for ladies.

Celia   Or I, I promise thee.

Rosalind   But is there any else longs to see this broken music in his
      sides? Is there yet another dotes upon rib breaking? Shall we see
      this wrestling, cousin?

Le Beau   You must if you stay here, for here is the place appointed for
      the wrestling, and they are ready to perform it.

Celia   Yonder, sure, they are coming. Let us now stay and see it.

Flourish. Enter Duke [Frederick], Lords,
Orlando, Charles, and attendants.

Duke Frederick   Come on. Since the youth will not be entreated, his
own peril on his forwardness.

Rosalind   Is yonder the man?

Le Beau   Even he, madam.

Celia   Alas, he is too young! Yet he looks successfully.

Duke Frederick   How now, daughter and cousin? Are you crept hither
to see the wrestling?

Rosalind   Ay, my liege, so please you give us leave.

Duke Frederick   You will take little delight in it, I can tell you, there is
such odds in the man. In pity of the challenger's youth I would fain
dissuade him, but he will not be entreated. Speak to him, ladies;
see if you can move him.

Celia   Call him hither, good Monsieur Le Beau.

Duke Frederick   Do so. I'll not be by.   [*He steps aside.*]

Le Beau [*to Orlando*]   Monsieur the challenger, the princess calls for
you.

Orlando [*approaching the ladies*]   I attend them with all respect and
duty.

Rosalind   Young man, have you challenged Charles the wrestler?

Orlando   No, fair princess. He is the general challenger. I come but
in, as others do, to try with him the strength of my youth.

Celia   Young gentleman, your spirits are too bold for your years. You
have seen cruel proof of this man's strength. If you saw yourself
with your eyes or knew yourself with your judgment, the fear of
your adventure would counsel you to a more equal enterprise. We
pray you, for your own sake, to embrace your own safety and give
over this attempt.

Rosalind   Do, young sir. Your reputation shall not therefore be misprized. We will make it our suit to the Duke that the wrestling
might not go forward.

Orlando   I beseech you, punish me not with your hard thoughts,
wherein I confess me much guilty to deny so fair and excellent ladies anything. But let your fair eyes and gentle wishes go with me

to my trial, wherein if I be foiled, there is but one shamed that was never gracious, if killed, but one dead that is willing to be so. I shall do my friends no wrong, for I have none to lament me; the world no injury, for in it I have nothing. Only in the world I fill up a place which may be better supplied when I have made it empty.

Rosalind   The little strength that I have, I would it were with you.

Celia   And mine, to eke out hers.

Rosalind   Fare you well. Pray heaven I be deceived in you!

Celia   Your heart's desires be with you!

Charles   Come, where is this young gallant that is so desirous to lie with his mother earth?

Orlando   Ready, sir, but his will hath in it a more modest working.

Duke Frederick   You shall try but one fall.

Charles   No, I warrant Your Grace, you shall not entreat him to a second, that have so mightily persuaded him from a first.

Orlando   You mean to mock me after; you should not have mocked me before. But come your ways.

Rosalind   Now Hercules be thy speed, young man!

Celia   I would I were invisible, to catch the strong fellow by the leg.

                            [*Orlando and Charles*] *wrestle.*

Rosalind   O excellent young man!

Celia   If I had a thunderbolt in mine eye, I can tell who should down.

                            Shout. [*Charles is thrown.*]

Duke Frederick   No more, no more.

Orlando   Yes, I beseech Your Grace. I am not yet well breathed.

Duke Frederick   How dost thou, Charles?

Le Beau   He cannot speak, my lord.

Duke Frederick   Bear him away. What is thy name, young man?

                            [*Charles is borne out.*]

Orlando   Orlando, my liege, the youngest son of Sir Rowland de Boys.

Duke Frederick

I would thou hadst been son to some man else.

The world esteemed thy father honorable,

But I did find him still mine enemy.

Thou shouldst have better pleased me with this deed

Hadst thou descended from another house.
But fare thee well; thou art a gallant youth.
I would thou hadst told me of another father.

> *Exit Duke [with train, and others. Rosalind and*
> *Celia remain; Orlando stands apart from them.]*

Celia [to Rosalind]
    Were I my father, coz, would I do this?
Orlando [to no one in particular]
    I am more proud to be Sir Rowland's son,
    His youngest son, and would not change that calling
    To be adopted heir to Frederick.
Rosalind [to Celia]
    My father loved Sir Rowland as his soul,
    And all the world was of my father's mind.
    Had I before known this young man his son,
    I should have given him tears unto entreaties
    Ere he should thus have ventured.
Celia [to Rosalind]   Gentle cousin,
    Let us go thank him and encourage him.
    My father's rough and envious disposition
    Sticks me at heart.—Sir, you have well deserved.
    If you do keep your promises in love
    But justly as you have exceeded all promise,
    Your mistress shall be happy.
Rosalind [giving him a chain from her neck]   Gentleman,
    Wear this for me, one out of suits with fortune,
    That could give more, but that her hand lacks means.
    [To Celia.] Shall we go, coz?
Celia   Ay. Fare you well, fair gentleman.
                        [Rosalind and Celia start to leave.]
Orlando [aside]
    Can I not say, "I thank you"? My better parts
    Are all thrown down, and that which here stands up
    Is but a quintain, a mere lifeless block.
Rosalind [to Celia]
    He calls us back. My pride fell with my fortunes;

I'll ask him what he would.—Did you call, sir?
Sir, you have wrestled well and overthrown
More than your enemies.

Celia   Will you go, coz?

Rosalind   Have with you.—Fare you well.

Exit [with Celia].

Orlando

What passion hangs these weights upon my tongue?
I cannot speak to her, yet she urged conference.
O poor Orlando, thou art overthrown!
Or Charles or something weaker masters thee.

Enter Le Beau.

Le Beau

Good sir, I do in friendship counsel you
To leave this place. Albeit you have deserved
High commendation, true applause, and love,
Yet such is now the Duke's condition
That he misconsters all that you have done.
The Duke is humorous. What he is indeed
More suits you to conceive than I to speak of.

Orlando

I thank you, sir. And, pray you, tell me this:
Which of the two was daughter of the Duke
That here was at the wrestling?

Le Beau

Neither his daughter, if we judge by manners,
But yet indeed the taller is his daughter.
The other is daughter to the banished Duke,
And here detained by her usurping uncle
To keep his daughter company, whose loves
Are dearer than the natural bond of sisters.
But I can tell you that of late this Duke
Hath ta'en displeasure gainst his gentle niece,
Grounded upon no other argument
But that the people praise her for her virtues

And pity her for her good father's sake;
And, on my life, his malice gainst the lady
Will suddenly break forth. Sir, fare you well.
Hereafter, in a better world than this,
I shall desire more love and knowledge of you.

Orlando

I rest much bounden to you. Fare you well.

[*Exit Le Beau.*]

Thus must I from the smoke into the smother,
From tyrant Duke unto a tyrant brother.
But heavenly Rosalind!

[*Exit.*]

1.3 ENTER CELIA AND ROSALIND.

Celia   Why, cousin, why, Rosalind! Cupid have mercy! Not a word?

Rosalind   Not one to throw at a dog.

Celia   No, thy words are too precious to be cast away upon curs. Throw some of them at me. Come, lame me with reasons.

Rosalind   Then there were two cousins laid up, when the one should be lamed with reasons and the other mad without any.

Celia   But is all this for your father?

Rosalind   No, some of it is for my child's father. O, how full of briers is this working-day world!

Celia   They are but burs, cousin, thrown upon thee in holiday foolery. If we walk not in the trodden paths, our very petticoats will catch them.

Rosalind   I could shake them off my coat. These burs are in my heart.

Celia   Hem them away.

Rosalind   I would try, if I could cry "hem" and have him.

Celia   Come, come, wrestle with thy affections.

Rosalind   O, they take the part of a better wrestler than myself.

Celia   O, a good wish upon you! You will try in time, in despite of a fall. But, turning these jests out of service, let us talk in good earnest. Is it possible, on such a sudden, you should fall into so strong a liking with old Sir Rowland's youngest son?

Rosalind   The Duke my father loved his father dearly.

Celia   Doth it therefore ensue that you should love his son dearly? By this kind of chase, I should hate him, for my father hated his father dearly; yet I hate not Orlando.

Rosalind   No, faith, hate him not, for my sake.

Celia   Why should I not? Doth he not deserve well?

Enter Duke [Frederick], with Lords.

Rosalind   Let me love him for that, and do you love him because I do.—Look, here comes the Duke.

Celia   With his eyes full of anger.

Duke Frederick [*to Rosalind*]
Mistress, dispatch you with your safest haste
And get you from our court.

Rosalind   Me, uncle?

Duke Frederick   You, cousin.
Within these ten days if that thou be'st found
So near our public court as twenty miles,
Thou diest for it.

Rosalind   I do beseech Your Grace
Let me the knowledge of my fault bear with me.
If with myself I hold intelligence
Or have acquaintance with mine own desires,
If that I do not dream or be not frantic—
As I do trust I am not—then, dear uncle,
Never so much as in a thought unborn
Did I offend Your Highness.

Duke Frederick   Thus do all traitors.
If their purgation did consist in words,
They are as innocent as grace itself.
Let it suffice thee that I trust thee not.

Rosalind
Yet your mistrust cannot make me a traitor.
Tell me whereon the likelihood depends.

Duke Frederick
Thou art thy father's daughter. There's enough.

Rosalind

So was I when Your Highness took his dukedom;
So was I when Your Highness banished him.
Treason is not inherited, my lord;
Or, if we did derive it from our friends,
What's that to me? My father was no traitor.
Then, good my liege, mistake me not so much
To think my poverty is treacherous.

Celia   Dear sovereign, hear me speak.

Duke Frederick

Ay, Celia, we stayed her for your sake,
Else had she with her father ranged along.

Celia

I did not then entreat to have her stay;
It was your pleasure and your own remorse.
I was too young that time to value her,
But now I know her. If she be a traitor,
Why, so am I. We still have slept together,
Rose at an instant, learned, played, eat together,
And wheresoe'er we went, like Juno's swans
Still we went coupled and inseparable.

Duke Frederick

She is too subtle for thee; and her smoothness,
Her very silence, and her patience
Speak to the people, and they pity her.
Thou art a fool. She robs thee of thy name,
And thou wilt show more bright and seem more virtuous
When she is gone. Then open not thy lips.
Firm and irrevocable is my doom
Which I have passed upon her; she is banished.

Celia

Pronounce that sentence then on me, my liege!
I cannot live out of her company.

Duke Frederick

You are a fool. You, niece, provide yourself.
If you outstay the time, upon mine honor,

And in the greatness of my word, you die.

Exit Duke [with Lords].

Celia

O my poor Rosalind, whither wilt thou go?
Wilt thou change fathers? I will give thee mine.
I charge thee, be not thou more grieved than I am.

Rosalind

I have more cause.

Celia   Thou hast not, cousin.
Prithee, be cheerful. Know'st thou not the Duke
Hath banished me, his daughter?

Rosalind   That he hath not.

Celia

No, hath not? Rosalind lacks then the love
Which teacheth thee that thou and I am one.
Shall we be sundered? Shall we part, sweet girl?
No, let my father seek another heir.
Therefore devise with me how we may fly,
Whither to go, and what to bear with us.
And do not seek to take your change upon you,
To bear your griefs yourself and leave me out;
For, by this heaven, now at our sorrows pale,
Say what thou canst, I'll go along with thee.

Rosalind   Why, whither shall we go?

Celia

To seek my uncle in the Forest of Arden.

Rosalind

Alas, what danger will it be to us,
Maids as we are, to travel forth so far!
Beauty provoketh thieves sooner than gold.

Celia

I'll put myself in poor and mean attire
And with a kind of umber smirch my face;
The like do you. So shall we pass along
And never stir assailants.

Rosalind   Were it not better,

Because that I am more than common tall,
That I did suit me all points like a man?
A gallant curtal ax upon my thigh,
A boar spear in my hand, and—in my heart
Lie there what hidden woman's fear there will—
We'll have a swashing and a martial outside,
As many other mannish cowards have
That do outface it with their semblances.

Celia

What shall I call thee when thou art a man?

Rosalind

I'll have no worse a name than Jove's own page,
And therefore look you call me Ganymede.
But what will you be called?

Celia

Something that hath a reference to my state:
No longer Celia, but Aliena.

Rosalind

But, cousin, what if we assayed to steal
The clownish fool out of your father's court?
Would he not be a comfort to our travel?

Celia

He'll go along o'er the wide world with me.
Leave me alone to woo him. Let's away,
And get our jewels and our wealth together,
Devise the fittest time and safest way
To hide us from pursuit that will be made
After my flight. Now go we in content
To liberty, and not to banishment.   [*Exeunt.*]

2.1 ENTER DUKE SENIOR, AMIENS, AND TWO OR THREE LORDS,
[DRESSED] LIKE FORESTERS.

Duke Senior

Now, my co-mates and brothers in exile,
Hath not old custom made this life more sweet

Than that of painted pomp? Are not these woods
More free from peril than the envious court?
Here feel we not the penalty of Adam,
The seasons' difference, as the icy fang
And churlish chiding of the winter's wind,
Which when it bites and blows upon my body
Even till I shrink with cold, I smile and say
"This is no flattery; these are counselors
That feelingly persuade me what I am."
Sweet are the uses of adversity,
Which, like the toad, ugly and venomous,
Wears yet a precious jewel in his head;
And this our life, exempt from public haunt,
Finds tongues in trees, books in the running brooks,
Sermons in stones, and good in everything.

Amiens

I would not change it. Happy is Your Grace
That can translate the stubbornness of fortune
Into so quiet and so sweet a style.

Duke Senior

Come, shall we go and kill us venison?
And yet it irks me the poor dappled fools,
Being native burghers of this desert city,
Should in their own confines with forkèd heads
Have their round haunches gored.

First Lord   Indeed, my lord,

The melancholy Jaques grieves at that,
And in that kind, swears you do more usurp
Than doth your brother that hath banished you.
Today my lord of Amiens and myself
Did steal behind him as he lay along
Under an oak whose antique root peeps out
Upon the brook that brawls along this wood,
To the which place a poor sequestered stag
That from the hunter's aim had ta'en a hurt

Did come to languish. And indeed, my lord,
The wretched animal heaved forth such groans
That their discharge did stretch his leathern coat
Almost to bursting, and the big round tears
Coursed one another down his innocent nose

In piteous chase. And thus the hairy fool,
Much markèd of the melancholy Jaques,
Stood on th' extremest verge of the swift brook,
Augmenting it with tears.

Duke Senior   But what said Jaques?
Did he not moralize this spectacle?

First Lord
O, yes, into a thousand similes.
First, for his weeping into the needless stream:
"Poor deer," quoth he, "thou mak'st a testament
As worldings do, giving thy sum of more
To that which had too much." Then, being there alone,
Left and abandoned of his velvet friends:
"'Tis right," quoth he, "thus misery doth part
The flux of company." Anon a careless herd,
Full of the pasture, jumps along by him
And never stays to greet him. "Ay," quoth Jaques,
"Sweep on, you fat and greasy citizens;
'Tis just the fashion. Wherefore do you look
Upon that poor and broken bankrupt there?"
Thus most invectively he pierceth through
The body of the country, city, court,
Yea, and of this our life, swearing that we
Are mere usurpers, tyrants, and what's worse,
To fright the animals and to kill them up
In their assigned and native dwelling place.

Duke Senior
And did you leave him in this contemplation?

Second Lord
We did, my lord, weeping and commenting
Upon the sobbing deer.

Duke Senior   Show me the place.
I love to cope him in these sullen fits,
For then he's full of matter.

First Lord   I'll bring you to him straight.   [*Exeunt.*]

2.2 ENTER DUKE [FREDERICK], WITH LORDS.

Duke Frederick
    Can it be possible that no man saw them?
    It cannot be. Some villains of my court
    Are of consent and sufferance in this.

First Lord
    I cannot hear of any that did see her.
    The ladies, her attendants of her chamber,
    Saw her abed, and in the morning early
    They found the bed untreasured of their mistress.

Second Lord
    My lord, the roynish clown, at whom so oft
    Your Grace was wont to laugh, is also missing.
    Hisperia, the princess' gentlewoman,
    Confesses that she secretly o'erheard
    Your daughter and her cousin much commend
    The parts and graces of the wrestler
    That did but lately foil the sinewy Charles,
    And she believes wherever they are gone
    That youth is surely in their company.

Duke Frederick
    Send to his brother. Fetch that gallant hither.
    If he be absent, bring his brother to me;
    I'll make him find him. Do this suddenly,
    And let not search and inquisition quail
    To bring again these foolish runaways.   *[Exeunt.]*

2.3 ENTER ORLANDO AND ADAM, [MEETING].

Orlando   Who's there?

Adam
    What, my young master? O my gentle master,
    O my sweet master, O you memory
    Of old Sir Rowland! Why, what make you here?

Why are you virtuous? Why do people love you?
And wherefore are you gentle, strong, and valiant?
Why would you be so fond to overcome
The bonny prizer of the humorous Duke?
Your praise is come too swiftly home before you.
Know you not, master, to some kind of men
Their graces serve them but as enemies?
No more do yours. Your virtues, gentle master,
Are sanctified and holy traitors to you.
O, what a world is this, when what is comely
Envenoms him that bears it!

Orlando
    Why, what's the matter?

Adam   O unhappy youth,
    Come not within these doors! Within this roof
The enemy of all your graces lives.
Your brother—no, no brother; yet the son—
Yet not the son, I will not call him son
Of him I was about to call his father—
Hath heard your praises, and this night he means
To burn the lodging where you use to lie
And you within it. If he fail of that,
He will have other means to cut you off.
I overheard him and his practices.
This is no place, this house is but a butchery.
Abhor it, fear it, do not enter it.

Orlando
    Why, whither, Adam, wouldst thou have me go?

Adam
    No matter whither, so you come not here.

Orlando
    What, wouldst thou have me go and beg my food?
Or with a base and boist'rous sword enforce
A thievish living on the common road?
This I must do or know not what to do;

Yet this I will not do, do how I can.
I rather will subject me to the malice
Of a diverted blood and bloody brother.

Adam

But do not so. I have five hundred crowns,
The thrifty hire I saved under your father,
Which I did store to be my foster nurse
When service should in my old limbs lie lame
And unregarded age in corners thrown.
Take that, and He that doth the ravens feed,
Yea, providently caters for the sparrow,
Be comfort to my age! Here is the gold;   [*offering gold*]
All this I give you. Let me be your servant.
Though I look old, yet I am strong and lusty,
For in my youth I never did apply
Hot and rebellious liquors in my blood,
Nor did not with unbashful forehead woo
The means of weakness and debility;
Therefore my age is as a lusty winter,
Frosty but kindly. Let me go with you.
I'll do the service of a younger man
In all your business and necessities.

Orlando

O good old man, how well in thee appears
The constant service of the antique world,
When service sweat for duty, not for meed!
Thou art not for the fashion of these times,
Where none will sweat but for promotion,
And having that do choke their service up
Even with the having. It is not so with thee.
But, poor old man, thou prun'st a rotten tree,
That cannot so much as a blossom yield
In lieu of all thy pains and husbandry.
But come thy ways. We'll go along together,
And ere we have thy youthful wages spent,

We'll light upon some settled low content.

Adam

Master, go on, and I will follow thee
To the last gasp, with truth and loyalty.
From seventeen years till now almost fourscore
Here livèd I, but now live here no more.
At seventeen years many their fortunes seek,
But at fourscore it is too late a week;
Yet fortune cannot recompense me better
Than to die well and not my master's debtor.

[*Exeunt.*]

2.4 ENTER ROSALIND FOR GANYMEDE, CELIA FOR ALIENA, AND CLOWN, ALIAS TOUCHSTONE.

Rosalind   O Jupiter, how weary are my spirits!

Touchstone   I care not for my spirits, if my legs were not weary.

Rosalind   I could find in my heart to disgrace my man's apparel and to cry like a woman; but I must comfort the weaker vessel, as doublet and hose ought to show itself courageous to petticoat. Therefore courage, good Aliena!

Celia   I pray you, bear with me. I cannot go no further.

Touchstone   For my part, I had rather bear with you than bear you; yet I should bear no cross if I did bear you, for I think you have no money in your purse.

Rosalind   Well, this is the Forest of Arden.

Touchstone   Ay, now am I in Arden; the more fool I. When I was at home I was in a better place, but travelers must be content.

Enter Corin and Silvius.

Rosalind   Ay, be so, good Touchstone.—Look you who comes here, a young man and an old in solemn talk.   [*They stand aside and listen.*]

Corin   That is the way to make her scorn you still.

Silvius   O Corin, that thou knew'st how I do love her!

Corin   I partly guess, for I have loved ere now.

Silvius

No, Corin, being old, thou canst not guess,
Though in thy youth thou wast as true a lover
As ever sighed upon a midnight pillow.
But if thy love were ever like to mine—
As sure I think did never man love so—

How many actions most ridiculous
Hast thou been drawn to by thy fantasy?
Corin

Into a thousand that I have forgotten.
Silvius

O, thou didst then never love so heartily!
If thou rememberest not the slightest folly
That ever love did make thee run into,
Thou hast not loved.
Or if thou hast not sat as I do now,
Wearing thy hearer in thy mistress' praise,
Thou hast not loved.
Or if thou hast not broke from company
Abruptly, as my passion now makes me,
Thou has not loved.
O Phoebe, Phoebe, Phoebe!   [*Exit.*]
Rosalind

Alas, poor shepherd! Searching of thy wound,
I have by hard adventure found mine own.
Touchstone   And I mine. I remember, when I was in love I broke my
sword upon a stone and bid him take that for coming a-night to
Jane Smile; and I remember the kissing of her batler and the cow's
dugs that her pretty chapped hands had milked; and I remember
the wooing of a peascod instead of her, from whom I took two
cods and, giving her them again, said with weeping tears, "Wear
these for my sake." We that are true lovers run into strange ca-
pers; but as all is mortal in nature, so is all nature in love mortal
in folly.
Rosalind   Thou speak'st wiser than thou art ware of.
Touchstone   Nay, I shall ne'er be ware of mine own wit till I break my
shins against it.
Rosalind

Jove, Jove! This shepherd's passion
Is much upon my fashion.
Touchstone

And mine, but it grows something stale with me.

Celia

    I pray you, one of you question yond man

    If he for gold will give us any food.

    I faint almost to death.

Touchstone [*to Corin*]   Holla: you, clown!

Rosalind

    Peace, Fool! He's not thy kinsman.

Corin   Who calls?

Touchstone

    Your betters, sir.

Corin   Else are they very wretched.

Rosalind

    Peace, I say.—Good even to you, friend.

Corin

    And to you, gentle sir, and to you all.

Rosalind

    I prithee, shepherd, if that love or gold

    Can in this desert place buy entertainment,

    Bring us where we may rest ourselves and feed.

    Here's a young maid with travel much oppressed,

    And faints for succor.

Corin   Fair sir, I pity her

    And wish, for her sake more than for mine own,

    My fortunes were more able to relieve her;

    But I am shepherd to another man

    And do not shear the fleeces that I graze.

    My master is of churlish disposition,

    And little recks to find the way to heaven

    By doing deeds of hospitality.

    Besides, his cote, his flocks, and bounds of feed

    Are now on sale, and at our sheepcote now,

    By reason of his absence, there is nothing

    That you will feed on. But what is, come see,

    And in my voice most welcome shall you be.

Rosalind

    What is he that shall buy his flock and pasture?

Corin

    That young swain that you saw here but erewhile,

    That little cares for buying anything.

Rosalind

    I pray thee, if it stand with honesty,

    Buy thou the cottage, pasture, and the flock,

    And thou shalt have to pay for it of us.

Celia

    And we will mend thy wages. I like this place

    And willingly could waste my time in it.

Corin

    Assuredly the thing is to be sold.

    Go with me. If you like upon report

    The soil, the profit, and this kind of life,

    I will your very faithful feeder be

    And buy it with your gold right suddenly.   [*Exeunt.*]

2.5 ENTER AMIENS, JAQUES, AND OTHERS.
[A TABLE IS SET OUT.]

Song.

Amiens [*sings*]

        Under the greenwood tree

        Who loves to lie with me,

        And turn his merry note

        Unto the sweet bird's throat,

    Come hither, come hither, come hither.

        Here shall he see

        No enemy

    But winter and rough weather.

Jaques   More, more, I prithee, more.

Amiens   It will make you melancholy, Monsieur Jaques.

Jaques   I thank it. More, I prithee, more. I can suck melancholy out of a song as a weasel sucks eggs. More, I prithee, more.

Amiens   My voice is ragged. I know I cannot please you.

Jaques I do not desire you to please me, I do desire you to sing. Come, more, another stanzo. Call you 'em "stanzos"?

Amiens What you will, Monsieur Jaques.

Jaques Nay, I care not for their names; they owe me nothing. Will you sing?

Amiens More at your request than to please myself.

Jaques Well then, if ever I thank any man, I'll thank you; but that they call "compliment" is like th' encounter of two dog-apes, and when a man thanks me heartily, methinks I have given him a penny and he renders me the beggarly thanks. Come, sing; and you that will not, hold your tongues.

Amiens Well, I'll end the song.—Sirs, cover the while; the Duke will drink under this tree.—He hath been all this day to look you.

[Food and drink are set out.]

Jaques And I have been all this day to avoid him. He is too disputable for my company. I think of as many matters as he, but I give heaven thanks and make no boast of them. Come, warble, come.

Song.

Amiens [*sings*]

      Who doth ambition shun
      And loves to live i' the sun,
      Seeking the food he eats
      And pleased with what he gets,

[All together here.]

   Come hither, come hither, come hither.
      Here shall he see
      No enemy
   But winter and rough weather.

Jaques I'll give you a verse to this note that I made yesterday in despite of my invention.

Amiens And I'll sing it.

Jaques Thus it goes:

      If it do come to pass
      That any man turn ass,

    Leaving his wealth and ease,
    A stubborn will to please,
  Ducdame, ducdame, ducdame.
    Here shall he see
    Gross fools as he,
  An if he will come to me.

Amiens   What's that "ducdame"?
Jaques   'Tis a Greek invocation, to call fools into a circle. I'll go sleep,
    if I can; if I cannot, I'll rail against all the firstborn of Egypt.
Amiens   And I'll go seek the Duke. His banquet is prepared.

                                                    Exeunt [separately].

2.6 ENTER ORLANDO AND ADAM.

Adam   Dear master, I can go no further. O, I die for food! Here lie I
    down and measure out my grave. Farewell, kind master.

                                                    [*He lies down.*]
Orlando   Why, how now, Adam? No greater heart in thee? Live a
    little, comfort a little, cheer thyself a little. If this uncouth forest
    yield anything savage, I will either be food for it or bring it for food
    to thee. Thy conceit is nearer death than thy powers. For my sake
    be comfortable; hold death awhile at the arm's end. I will here be
    with thee presently, and if I bring thee not something to eat, I will
    give thee leave to die; but if thou diest before I come, thou art a
    mocker of my labor. Well said! Thou look'st cheerly, and I'll be
    with thee quickly. Yet thou liest in the bleak air. Come, I will bear
    thee to some shelter; and thou shalt not die for lack of a dinner, if
    there live anything in this desert. [*He picks up Adam.*] Cheerly, good
    Adam!   [*Exeunt.*]

2.7 ENTER DUKE SENIOR AND LORDS, LIKE OUTLAWS.

Duke Senior
  I think he be transformed into a beast,
  For I can nowhere find him like a man.

First Lord

    My lord, he is but even now gone hence.

    Here was he merry, hearing of a song.

Duke Senior

    If he, compact of jars, grow musical,

    We shall have shortly discord in the spheres.

    Go seek him. Tell him I would speak with him.

Enter Jaques.

First Lord

    He saves my labor by his own approach.

Duke Senior

    Why, how now, monsieur, what a life is this,

    That your poor friends must woo your company!

    What, you look merrily.

Jaques

    A fool, a fool! I met a fool i' the forest,

    A motley fool. A miserable world!

    As I do live by food, I met a fool,

    Who laid him down and basked him in the sun,

    And railed on Lady Fortune in good terms,

    In good set terms, and yet a motley fool.

    "Good morrow, Fool," quoth I. "No, sir," quoth he,

    "Call me not fool till heaven hath sent me fortune."

    And then he drew a dial from his poke

    And, looking on it with lackluster eye,

    Says very wisely, "It is ten o'clock.

    Thus we may see," quoth he, "how the world wags.

    'Tis but an hour ago since it was nine,

    And after one hour more 'twill be eleven;

    And so from hour to hour we ripe and ripe,

    And then from hour to hour we rot and rot,

    And thereby hangs a tale." When I did hear

    The motley fool thus moral on the time,

    My lungs began to crow like Chanticleer,

    That fools should be so deep-contemplative,

And I did laugh sans intermission
An hour by his dial. O noble fool!
A worthy fool! Motley's the only wear.

Duke Senior

What fool is this?

Jaques

O worthy fool! One that hath been a courtier,
And says, if ladies be but young and fair,
They have the gift to know it. And in his brain,
Which is as dry as the remainder biscuit
After a voyage, he hath strange places crammed
With observation, the which he vents
In mangled forms. O, that I were a fool!
I am ambitious for a motley coat.

Duke Senior

Thou shalt have one.

Jaques   It is my only suit,
Provided that you weed your better judgments
Of all opinion that grows rank in them
That I am wise. I must have liberty
Withal, as large a charter as the wind,
To blow on whom I please, for so fools have.
And they that are most gallèd with my folly,
They most must laugh. And why, sir, must they so?
The "why" is plain as way to parish church:
He that a fool doth very wisely hit
Doth very foolishly, although he smart,
Not to seem senseless of the bob. If not,
The wise man's folly is anatomized
Even by the squand'ring glances of the fool.
Invest me in my motley; give me leave
To speak my mind, and I will through and through
Cleanse the foul body of th' infected world,
If they will patiently receive my medicine.

Duke Senior

Fie on thee! I can tell what thou wouldst do.

Jaques
   What, for a counter, would I do but good?
Duke Senior
   Most mischievous foul sin, in chiding sin.
   For thou thyself hast been a libertine,
   As sensual as the brutish sting itself;
   And all th' embossèd sores and headed evils
   That thou with license of free foot hast caught
   Wouldst thou disgorge into the general world.
Jaques   Why, who cries out on pride
   That can therein tax any private party?
   Doth it not flow as hugely as the sea,
   Till that the weary very means do ebb?
   What woman in the city do I name,
   When that I say the city woman bears
   The cost of princes on unworthy shoulders?
   Who can come in and say that I mean her,
   When such a one as she, such is her neighbor?
   Or what is he of basest function
   That says his bravery is not on my cost,
   Thinking that I mean him, but therein suits
   His folly to the mettle of my speech?
   There then, how then? What then? Let me see wherein
   My tongue hath wronged him. If it do him right,
   Then he hath wronged himself. If he be free,
   Why then my taxing like a wild goose flies,
   Unclaimed of any man.—But who comes here?

                Enter Orlando [with his sword drawn].

Orlando
   Forbear, and eat no more!
Jaques   Why, I have eat none yet.
Orlando
   Nor shalt not, till necessity be served.
Jaques
   Of what kind should this cock come of?

Duke Senior

 Art thou thus boldened, man, by thy distress,
 Or else a rude despiser of good manners,
 That in civility thou seem'st so empty?

Orlando

 You touched my vein at first. The thorny point
 Of bare distress hath ta'en from me the show
 Of smooth civility; yet am I inland bred
 And know some nurture. But forbear, I say.
 He dies that touches any of this fruit
 Till I and my affairs are answerèd.

Jaques

 An you will not be answered with reason, I must die.

Duke Senior

 What would you have? Your gentleness shall force
 More than your force move us to gentleness.

Orlando

 I almost die for food, and let me have it!

Duke Senior

 Sit down and feed, and welcome to our table.

Orlando

 Speak you so gently? Pardon me, I pray you.
 I thought that all things had been savage here,
 And therefore put I on the countenance
 Of stern commandment. But whate'er you are
 That in this desert inaccessible,
 Under the shade of melancholy boughs,
 Lose and neglect the creeping hours of time;
 If ever you have looked on better days,
 If ever been where bells have knolled to church,
 If ever sat at any good man's feast,
 If ever from your eyelids wiped a tear
 And know what 'tis to pity and be pitied,
 Let gentleness my strong enforcement be,
 In the which hope I blush and hide my sword.

          [He sheathes his sword.]

Duke Senior

    True is it that we have seen better days,
    And have with holy bell been knolled to church,
    And sat at good men's feasts, and wiped our eyes
    Of drops that sacred pity hath engendered.
    And therefore sit you down in gentleness,
    And take upon command what help we have
    That to your wanting may be ministered.

Orlando

    Then but forbear your food a little while,
    Whiles, like a doe, I go to find my fawn
    And give it food. There is an old poor man
    Who after me hath many a weary step
    Limped in pure love. Till he be first sufficed,
    Oppressed with two weak evils, age and hunger,
    I will not touch a bit.

Duke Senior   Go find him out,
    And we will nothing waste till you return.

Orlando

    I thank ye; and be blest for your good comfort!

                                                [Exit.]

Duke Senior

    Thou seest we are not all alone unhappy.
    This wide and universal theater
    Presents more woeful pageants than the scene
    Wherein we play in.

Jaques   All the world's a stage,
    And all the men and women merely players.
    They have their exits and their entrances,
    And one man in his time plays many parts,
    His acts being seven ages. At first the infant,
    Mewling and puking in the nurse's arms.
    Then the whining schoolboy, with his satchel
    And shining morning face, creeping like snail
    Unwillingly to school. And then the lover,
    Sighing like furnace, with a woeful ballad

Made to his mistress' eyebrow. Then a soldier,
Full of strange oaths and bearded like the pard,
Jealous in honor, sudden, and quick in quarrel,
Seeking the bubble reputation
Even in the cannon's mouth. And then the justice,
In fair round belly with good capon lined,
With eyes severe and beard of formal cut,
Full of wise saws and modern instances;
And so he plays his part. The sixth age shifts
Into the lean and slippered pantaloon,
With spectacles on nose and pouch on side,
His youthful hose, well saved, a world too wide
For his shrunk shank; and his big manly voice,
Turning again toward childish treble, pipes
And whistles in his sound. Last scene of all,
That ends this strange, eventful history,
Is second childishness and mere oblivion,
Sans teeth, sans eyes, sans taste, sans everything.

Enter Orlando, with Adam.

Duke Senior
    Welcome. Set down your venerable burden
    And let him feed.
Orlando   I thank you most for him.

[He sets down Adam.]

Adam   So had you need.
    I scarce can speak to thank you for myself.
Duke Senior
    Welcome. Fall to. I will not trouble you
    As yet to question you about your fortunes.—
    Give us some music, and, good cousin, sing.

*[They eat, while Orlando and
Duke Senior converse apart.]*

Song.

Amiens [*sings*]
        Blow, blow, thou winter wind.

Thou art not so unkind
　　As man's ingratitude.
Thy tooth is not so keen,
Because thou art not seen,
　　Although thy breath be rude.
Heigh-ho, sing heigh-ho, unto the green holly.
Most friendship is feigning, most loving mere folly.
　　Then heigh-ho, the holly!
　　　　This life is most jolly.
Freeze, freeze, thou bitter sky,
That dost not bite so nigh
　　As benefit's forgot.
Though thou the waters warp,
Thy sting is not so sharp
　　As friend remembered not.
Heigh-ho, sing heigh-ho, unto the green holly.
Most friendship is feigning, most loving mere folly.
　　Then heigh-ho, the holly!
　　　　This life is most jolly.

Duke Senior [*to Orlando*]
　　If that you were the good Sir Rowland's son,
　　As you have whispered faithfully you were
　　And as mine eye doth his effigies witness
　　Most truly limned and living in your face,
　　Be truly welcome hither. I am the Duke
　　That loved your father. The residue of your fortune,
　　Go to my cave and tell me.—Good old man,
　　Thou art right welcome as thy master is.—
　　Support him by the arm. Give me your hand,
　　And let me all your fortunes understand.　　　　　　[*Exeunt.*]

3.1 ENTER DUKE [FREDERICK], LORDS, AND OLIVER.

Duke Frederick
　　Not see him since? Sir, sir, that cannot be.

But were I not the better part made mercy,
I should not seek an absent argument
Of my revenge, thou present. But look to it:
Find out thy brother, wheresoe'er he is.
Seek him with candle. Bring him dead or living
Within this twelvemonth, or turn thou no more
To seek a living in our territory.
Thy lands and all things that thou dost call thine
Worth seizure do we seize into our hands,
Till thou canst quit thee by thy brother's mouth
Of what we think against thee.

Oliver

O, that Your Highness knew my heart in this!
I never loved my brother in my life.

Duke Frederick

More villain thou.—Well, push him out of doors,
And let my officers of such a nature
Make an extent upon his house and lands.
Do this expediently, and turn him going.   [*Exeunt.*]

3.2 ENTER ORLANDO [*WITH A PAPER*].

Orlando

Hang there, my verse, in witness of my love;
    And thou, thrice-crownèd queen of night, survey
With thy chaste eye, from thy pale sphere above,
    Thy huntress' name that my full life doth sway.
O Rosalind! These trees shall be my books,
    And in their barks my thoughts I'll character,
That every eye which in this forest looks
    Shall see thy virtue witnessed everywhere.
Run, run, Orlando, carve on every tree
The fair, the chaste, and unexpressive she.   [*Exit.*]

Enter Corin and [Touchstone the] Clown.

Corin   And how like you this shepherd's life, Master Touchstone?

Touchstone Truly, shepherd, in respect of itself, it is a good life; but in respect that it is a shepherd's life, it is naught. In respect that it is solitary, I like it very well; but in respect that it is private, it is a very vile life. Now in respect it is in the fields, it pleaseth me well; but in respect it is not in the court, it is tedious. As it is a spare life, look you, it fits my humor well; but as there is no more plenty in it, it goes much against my stomach. Hast any philosophy in thee, shepherd?

Corin No more but that I know the more one sickens the worse at ease he is; and that he that wants money, means, and content is without three good friends; that the property of rain is to wet and fire to burn; that good pasture makes fat sheep and that a great cause of the night is lack of the sun; that he that hath learned no wit by nature nor art may complain of good breeding or comes of a very dull kindred.

Touchstone Such a one is a natural philosopher. Wast ever in court, shepherd?

Corin No, truly.

Touchstone   Then thou art damned.

Corin   Nay, I hope.

Touchstone   Truly, thou art damned, like an ill-roasted egg, all on one side.

Corin   For not being at court? Your reason.

Touchstone   Why, if thou never wast at court, thou never sawst good manners; if thou never sawst good manners, then thy manners must be wicked; and wickedness is sin, and sin is damnation. Thou art in a parlous state, shepherd.

Corin   Not a whit, Touchstone. Those that are good manners at the court are as ridiculous in the country as the behavior of the country is most mockable at me court. You told me you salute not at the court but you kiss your hands; that courtesy would be uncleanly, if courtiers were shepherds.

Touchstone   Instance, briefly; come, instance.

Corin   Why, we are still handling our ewes, and their fells you know are greasy.

Touchstone   Why, do not your courtier's hands sweat? And is not the grease of a mutton as wholesome as the sweat of a man? Shallow, shallow. A better instance, I say. Come.

Corin   Besides, our hands are hard.

Touchstone   Your lips will feel them the sooner. Shallow again. A more sounder instance. Come.

Corin   And they are often tarred over with the surgery of our sheep; and would you have us kiss tar? The courtier's hands are perfumed with civet.

Touchstone   Most shallow man! Thou worms'meat, in respect of a good piece of flesh indeed! Learn of the wise, and perpend: civet is of a baser birth than tar, the very uncleanly flux of a cat. Mend the instance, shepherd.

Corin   You have too courtly a wit for me. I'll rest.

Touchstone   Wilt thou rest damned? God help thee, shallow man! God make incision in thee! Thou art raw.

Corin   Sir, I am a true laborer: I earn that I eat, get that I wear, owe no man hate, envy no man's happiness, glad of other men's good,

content with my harm, and the greatest of my pride is to see my
ewes graze and my lambs suck.

Touchstone   That is another simple sin in you, to bring the ewes and
the rams together and to offer to get your living by the copulation
of cattle; to be bawd to a bellwether, and to betray a she-lamb of a
twelvemonth to a crooked-pated old cuckoldlyram, out of all reasonable match. If thou beest not damned for this, the devil himself
will have no shepherds; I cannot see else how thou shouldst scape.

Corin   Here comes young Master Ganymede, my new mistress's
brother.

Enter Rosalind [with a paper, reading].

Rosalind
"From the east to western Ind,
No jewel is like Rosalind.
Her worth, being mounted on the wind,
Through all the world bears Rosalind.
All the pictures fairest lined
Are but black to Rosalind.
Let no face be kept in mind
But the fair of Rosalind."

Touchstone   I'll rhyme you so eight years together, dinners and sup-
pers and sleeping hours excepted. It is the right butter-women's
rank to market.

Rosalind   Out, fool!

Touchstone   For a taste:
If a hart do lack a hind,
Let him seek out Rosalind.
If the cat will after kind,
So, be sure, will Rosalind.
Wintered garments must be lined,
So must slender Rosalind.
They that reap must sheaf and bind;
Then to cart with Rosalind.

Sweetest nut hath sourest rind;
Such a nut is Rosalind.
He that sweetest rose will find
Must find love's prick and Rosalind.

This is the very false gallop of verses. Why do you infect yourself
with them?

Rosalind   Peace, you dull fool! I found them on a tree.

Touchstone   Truly, the tree yields bad fruit.

Rosalind   I'll graft it with you, and then I shall graft it with a medlar. Then it will be the earliest fruit i' the country; for you'll be rotten ere you be half ripe, and that's the right virtue of the medlar.

Touchstone   You have said; but whether wisely or no, let the forest judge.

Enter Celia, with a writing.

Rosalind   Peace! Here comes my sister, reading. Stand aside.

Celia [*reads*]

> "Why should this a desert be?
>   For it is unpeopled? No.
> Tongues I'll hang on every tree,
>   That shall civil sayings show:
> Some, how brief the life of man
>   Runs his erring pilgrimage,
> That the stretching of a span
>   Buckles in his sum of age;
> Some, of violated vows
>   Twixt the souls of friend and friend;
> But upon the fairest boughs,
>   Or at every sentence end,
> Will I 'Rosalinda' write,
>   Teaching all that read to know
> The quintessence of every sprite
>   Heaven would in little show.
> Therefore heaven Nature charged
>   That one body should be filled
> With all graces wide-enlarged.
>   Nature presently distilled
> Helen's cheek, but not her heart,
>   Cleopatra's majesty,
> Atalanta's better part,
>   Sad Lucretia's modesty.

Thus Rosalind of many parts
      By heavenly synod was devised
Of many faces, eyes, and hearts
      To have the touches dearest prized.
Heaven would that she these gifts should have,
And I to live and die her slave."

Rosalind   O most gentle Jupiter, what tedious homily of love have you
      wearied your parishioners withal, and never cried, "Have patience,
      good people!"
Celia   How now? Back, friends. Shepherd, go off a little. [*To Touchstone.*]
      Go with him, sirrah.
Touchstone   Come, shepherd, let us make an honorable retreat,
      though not with bag and baggage, yet with scrip and scrippage.

                                                  Exit [with Corin].

Celia   Didst thou hear these verses?
Rosalind   O, yes, I heard them all, and more, too, for some of them
      had in them more feet than the verses would bear.
Celia   That's no matter. The feet might bear the verses.
Rosalind   Ay, but the feet were lame and could not bear themselves
      without the verse and therefore stood lamely in the verse.
Celia   But didst thou hear without wondering how thy name should
      be hanged and carved upon these trees?
Rosalind   I was seven of the nine days out of the wonder before you
      came; for look here what I found on a palm tree. I was never so be-
      rhymed since Pythagoras' time, that I was an Irish rat, which I can
      hardly remember.
Celia   Trow you who hath done this?
Rosalind   Is it a man?
Celia   And a chain that you once wore about his neck. Change you
      color?
Rosalind   I prithee, who?
Celia   O Lord, Lord, it is a hard matter for friends to meet; but moun-
      tains may be removed with earthquakes and so encounter.
Rosalind   Nay, but who is it?
Celia   Is it possible?

Rosalind   Nay, I prithee now with most petitionary vehemence, tell me who it is.

Celia   O wonderful, wonderful, and most wonderful wonderful! And yet again wonderful, and after that, out of all whooping!

Rosalind   Good my complexion! Dost thou think, though I am caparisoned like a man, I have a doublet and hose in my disposition? One inch of delay more is a South Sea of discovery. I prithee, tell me who is it quickly, and speak apace. I would thou couldst stammer, that thou mightst pour this concealed man out of thy mouth as wine comes out of a narrow-mouthed bottle, either too much at once or none at all. I prithee, take the cork out of thy mouth that I may drink thy tidings.

Celia   So you may put a man in your belly.

Rosalind   Is he of God's making? What manner of man? Is his head worth a hat, or his chin worth a beard?

Celia   Nay, he hath but a little beard.

Rosalind   Why, God will send more, if the man will be thankful. Let me stay the growth of his beard, if thou delay me not the knowledge of his chin.

Celia   It is young Orlando, that tripped up the wrestler's heels and your heart both in an instant.

Rosalind   Nay, but the devil take mocking. Speak sad brow and true maid.

Celia   I' faith, coz, 'tis he.

Rosalind   Orlando?

Celia   Orlando.

Rosalind   Alas the day, what shall I do with my doublet and hose? What did he when thou sawst him? What said he? How looked he? Wherein went he? What makes he here? Did he ask for me? Where remains he? How parted he with thee? And when shalt thou see him again? Answer me in one word.

Celia   You must borrow me Gargantua's mouth first; 'tis a word too great for any mouth of this age's size. To say ay and no to these particulars is more than to answer in a catechism.

Rosalind   But doth he know that I am in this forest and in man's apparel? Looks he as freshly as he did the day he wrestled?

Celia   It is as easy to count atomies as to resolve the propositions of
a lover. But take a taste of my finding him, and relish it with good
observance. I found him under a tree, like a dropped acorn.

Rosalind   It may well be called Jove's tree, when it drops forth such
fruit.

Celia   Give me audience, good madam.

Rosalind   Proceed.

Celia   There lay he, stretched along, like a wounded knight.

Rosalind   Though it be pity to see such a sight, it well becomes the
ground.

Celia   Cry "holla" to thy tongue, I prithee; it curvets unseasonably.
He was furnished like a hunter.

Rosalind   O, ominous! He comes to kill my heart.

Celia   I would sing my song without a burden. Thou bring'st me out
of tune.

Rosalind   Do you not know I am a woman? When I think, I must
speak. Sweet, say on.

Enter Orlando and Jaques.

Celia   You bring me out.—Soft, comes he not here?

Rosalind   'Tis he. Slink by, and note him.

[*They stand aside and listen.*]

Jaques [*to Orlando*]   I thank you for your company, but, good faith, I
had as lief have been myself alone.

Orlando   And so had I; but yet, for fashion's sake, I thank you too for
your society.

Jaques   God b' wi' you. Let's meet as little as we can.

Orlando   I do desire we may be better strangers.

Jaques   I pray you, mar no more trees with writing love songs in their
barks.

Orlando   I pray you, mar no more of my verses with reading them
ill-favoredly.

Jaques   Rosalind is your love's name?

Orlando   Yes, just.

Jaques   I do not like her name.

Orlando There was no thought of pleasing you when she was christened.

Jaques What stature is she of?

Orlando Just as high as my heart.

Jaques You are full of pretty answers. Have you not been acquainted with goldsmiths' wives, and conned them out of rings?

Orlando Not so; but I answer you right painted cloth, from whence you have studied your questions.

Jaques You have a nimble wit; I think 'twas made of Atalanta's heels. Will you sit down with me? And we two will rail against our mistress the world and all our misery.

Orlando I will chide no breather in the world but myself, against whom I know most faults.

Jaques The worst fault you have is to be in love.

Orlando 'Tis a fault I will not change for your best virtue. I am weary of you.

Jaques By my troth, I was seeking for a fool when I found you.

Orlando He is drowned in the brook. Look but in, and you shall see him.

Jaques There I shall see mine own figure.

Orlando Which I take to be either a fool or a cipher.

Jaques I'll tarry no longer with you. Farewell, good Seigneur Love.

Orlando I am glad of your departure. Adieu, good Monsieur Melancholy.   [*Exit Jaques.*]

Rosalind [*aside to Celia*] I will speak to him like a saucy lackey and under that habit play the knave with him.—Do you hear, forester?

Orlando Very well. What would you?

Rosalind I pray you, what is 't o'clock?

Orlando You should ask me what time o' day. There's no clock in the forest.

Rosalind Then there is no true lover in the forest, else sighing every minute and groaning every hour would detect the lazy foot of Time as well as a clock.

Orlando And why not the swift foot of Time? Had not that been as proper?

Rosalind   By no means, sir. Time travels in divers paces with divers persons. I'll tell you who Time ambles withal, who Time trots withal, who Time gallops withal, and who he stands still withal.

Orlando   I prithee, who doth lie trot withal?

Rosalind   Marry, he trots hard with a young maid between the con-tract of her marriage and the day it is solemnized. If the interim be but a se'nnight, Time's pace is so hard that it seems the length of seven year.

Orlando   Who ambles Time withal?

Rosalind   With a priest that lacks Latin and a rich man that hath not the gout, for the one sleeps easily because he cannot study and the other lives merrily because he feels no pain, the one lacking the burden of lean and wasteful learning, the other knowing no burden of heavy tedious penury. These Time ambles withal.

Orlando   Who doth he gallop withal?

Rosalind   With a thief to the gallows, for though he go as softly as foot can fall, he thinks himself too soon there.

Orlando   Who stays it still withal?

Rosalind   With lawyers in the vacation; for they sleep between term and term, and then they perceive not how Time moves.

Orlando   Where dwell you, pretty youth?

Rosalind   With this shepherdess, my sister, here in the skirts of the forest, like fringe upon a petticoat.

Orlando   Are you native of this place?

Rosalind   As the coney that you see dwell where she is kindled.

Orlando   Your accent is something finer than you could purchase in so removed a dwelling.

Rosalind   I have been told so of many. But indeed an old religious uncle of mine taught me to speak, who was in his youth an inland man, one that knew courtship too well, for there he fell in love. I have heard him read many lectures against it, and I thank God I am not a woman, to be touched with so many giddy offences as he hath generally taxed their whole sex withal.

Orlando   Can you remember any of the principal evils that he laid to the charge of women?

Rosalind   There were none principal; they were all like one another as halfpence are, every one fault seeming monstrous till his fellow fault came to match it.

Orlando   I prithee, recount some of them.

Rosalind   No, I will not cast away my physic but on those that are sick. There is a man haunts the forest that abuses our young plants with carving "Rosalind" on. their barks, hangs odes upon hawthorns and elegies on brambles, all, forsooth, deifying the name of Rosalind. If I could meet that fancy-monger, I would give him some good counsel, for he seems to have the quotidian of love upon him.

Orlando   I am he that is so love-shaked. I pray you, tell me your remedy.

Rosalind   There is none of my uncle's marks upon you. He taught me how to know a man in love, in which cage of rushes I am sure you are not prisoner.

Orlando   What were his marks?

Rosalind   A lean cheek, which you have not; a blue eye and sunken, which you have not; an unquestionable spirit, which you have not; a beard neglected, which you have not—but I pardon you for that, for simply your having in beard is a younger brother's revenue. Then your hose should be ungartered, your bonnet unbanded, your sleeve unbuttoned, your shoe untied, and everything about you demonstrating a careless desolation. But you are no such man. You are rather point-device in your accoutrements, as loving yourself, than seeming the lover of any other.

Orlando   Fair youth, I would I could make thee believe I love.

Rosalind   Me believe it? You may as soon make her that you love believe it, which I warrant she is apter to do than to confess she does. That is one of the points in the which women still give the lie to their consciences. But in good sooth, are you he that hangs the verses on the trees, wherein Rosalind is so admired?

Orlando   I swear to thee, youth, by the white hand of Rosalind, I am that he, that unfortunate he.

Rosalind   But are you so much in love as your rhymes speak?

Orlando   Neither rhyme nor reason can express how much.

Rosalind   Love is merely a madness and, I tell you, deserves as well a
dark house and a whip as madmen do; and the reason why they are
not so punished and cured is that the lunacy is so ordinary that the
whippers are in love too. Yet I profess curing it by counsel.

Orlando   Did you ever cure any so?

Rosalind   Yes, one, and in this manner. He was to imagine me his
love, his mistress; and I set him every day to woo me. At which time
would I, being but a moonish youth, grieve, be effeminate, change-
able, longing and liking, proud, fantastical, apish, shallow, inconstant, full of tears, full of smiles; for every passion something and
for no passion truly anything, as boys and women are for the most
part cattle of this color; would now like him, now loathe him; then
entertain him, then forswear him; now weep for him, then spit at
him; that I drave my suitor from his mad humor of love to a living
humor of madness, which was to forswear the full stream of the
world and to live in a nook merely monastic. And thus I cured him;
and this way will I take upon me to wash your liver as clean as a
sound sheep's heart, that there shall not be one spot of love in 't.

Orlando   I would not be cured, youth.

Rosalind   I would cure you, if you would but call me Rosalind and
come every day to my cote and woo me.

Orlando   Now by the faith of my love, I will. Tell me where it is.

Rosalind   Go with me to it, and I'll show it you; and by the way you
shall tell me where in the forest you live. Will you go?

Orlando   With all my heart, good youth.

Rosalind   Nay, you must call me Rosalind.—Come, sister, will you
go?   [*Exeunt.*]

3.3 ENTER [TOUCHSTONE THE] CLOWN, AUDREY; AND
JAQUES [APART].

Touchstone   Come apace, good Audrey. I will fetch up your goats,
Audrey. And how, Audrey, am I the man yet? Doth my simple fea-
ture content you?

Audrey   Your features, Lord warrant us! What features?

Touchstone I am here with thee and thy goats, as the most capricious poet, honest Ovid, was among the Goths.

Jaques [*aside*] O knowledge ill-inhabited, worse than Jove in a thatched house!

Touchstone When a man's verses cannot be understood, nor a man's good wit seconded with the forward child, understanding, it strikes a man more dead than a great reckoning in a little room. Truly, I would the gods had made thee poetical.

Audrey I do not know what "poetical" is. Is it honest in deed and word? Is it a true thing?

Touchstone No, truly; for the truest poetry is the most feigning, and lovers are given to poetry, and what they swear in poetry may be said as lovers they do feign.

Audrey Do you wish then that the gods had made me poetical?

Touchstone I do, truly; for thou swear'st to me thou art honest. Now, if thou wert a poet, I might have some hope thou didst feign.

Audrey Would you not have me honest?

Touchstone No, truly, unless thou wert hard-favored; for honesty coupled to beauty is to have honey a sauce to sugar.

Jaques [*aside*] A material fool!

Audrey Well, I am not fair, and therefore I pray the gods make me honest.

Touchstone Truly, and to cast away honesty upon a foul slut were to put good meat into an unclean dish.

Audrey I am not a slut, though I thank the gods I am foul.

Touchstone Well, praised be the gods for thy foulness! Sluttishness may come hereafter. But be it as it may be, I will marry thee, and to that end I have been with Sir Oliver Mar-text, the vicar of the next village, who hath promised to meet me in this place of the forest and to couple us.

Jaques [*aside*] I would fain see this meeting.

Audrey Well, the gods give us joy!

Touchstone Amen. A man may, if he were of a fearful heart, stagger in this attempt; for here we have no temple but the wood, no assembly but horn-beasts. But what though? Courage! As horns are odious, they are necessary. It is said, "Many a man knows no end of his goods." Right! Many a man has good horns and knows no end of them. Well, that is the dowry of his wife; 'tis none of his own getting. Horns? Even so. Poor men alone? No, no, the noblest deer hath them as huge as the rascal. Is the single man therefore blessed? No. As a walled town is more worthier than a village, so is the forehead of a married man more honorable than the bare brow of a bachelor; and by how much defense is better than no skill, by so much is a horn more precious than to want.

Enter Sir Oliver Mar-text.

Here comes Sir Oliver. Sir Oliver Mar-text, you are well met. Will you dispatch us here under this tree, or shall we go with you to your chapel?

Sir Oliver   Is there none here to give the woman?

Touchstone   I will not take her on gift of any man.

Sir Oliver   Truly, she must be given, or the marriage is not lawful.

Jaques [*advancing*]   Proceed, proceed. I'll give her.

Touchstone   Good even, good Master What-ye-call-'t. How do you, sir? You are very well met. God 'ild you for your last company. I am very glad to see you. Even a toy in hand here, sir.—Nay, pray be covered.

Jaques   Will you be married, motley?

Touchstone   As the ox hath his bow, sir, the horse his curb, and the falcon her bells, so man hath his desires; and as pigeons bill, so wedlock would be nibbling.

Jaques   And will you, being a man of your breeding, be married under a bush like a beggar? Get you to church, and have a good priest that can tell you what marriage is. This fellow will but join you together as they join wainscot; then one of you will prove a shrunk panel and, like green timber, warp, warp.

Touchstone   I am not in the mind but I were better to be married of him than of another, for he is not like to marry me well; and not being well married, it will be a good excuse for me hereafter to leave my wife.

Jaques   Go thou with me, and let me counsel thee.

Touchstone   Come, sweet Audrey. We must be married, or we must live in bawdry. Farewell, good Master Oliver; not

> "O sweet Oliver,
> O brave Oliver,
> Leave me not behind thee";

but

> "Wind away,
> Begone, I say,
> I will not to wedding with thee."

> > *[Exeunt Jaques, Touchstone, and Audrey.]*

Sir Oliver   'Tis no matter. Ne'er a fantastical knave of them all shall flout me out of my calling.   *[Exit.]*

3.4 ENTER ROSALIND AND CELIA.

Rosalind   Never talk to me. I will weep.

Celia   Do, I prithee, but yet have the grace to consider that tears do not become a man.

Rosalind   But have I not cause to weep?

Celia   As good cause as one would desire; therefore weep.

Rosalind   His very hair is of the dissembling color.

Celia   Something browner than Judas's. Marry, his kisses are Judas's own children.

Rosalind   I' faith, his hair is of a good color.

Celia   An excellent color. Your chestnut was ever the only color.

Rosalind   And his kissing is as full of sanctity as the touch of holy bread.

Celia   He hath bought a pair of cast lips of Diana. A nun of winter's sisterhood kisses not more religiously; the very ice of chastity is in them.

Rosalind   But why did he swear he would come this morning, and comes not?

Celia   Nay, certainly, there is no truth in him.

Rosalind   Do you think so?

Celia   Yes. I think he is not a pickpurse nor a horse-stealer, but for his verity in love, I do think him as concave as a covered goblet or a worm-eaten nut.

Rosalind   Not true in love?

Celia   Yes, when he is in, but I think he is not in.

Rosalind   You have heard him swear downright he was.

Celia   "Was" is not "is." Besides, the oath of a lover is no stronger than the word of a tapster; they are both the confirmer of false reckonings. He attends here in the forest on the Duke your father.

Rosalind   I met the Duke yesterday and had much question with him. He asked me of what parentage I was. I told him, of as good as he;

so he laughed and let me go. But what talk we of fathers, when there is such a man as Orlando?

Celia O, that's a brave man! He writes brave verses, speaks brave words, swears brave oaths, and breaks them bravely, quite traverse, athwart the heart of his lover, as a puny tilter, that spurs his horse but on one side, breaks his staff like a noble goose. But all's brave that youth mounts and folly guides. Who comes here?

Enter Corin.

Corin
Mistress and master, you have oft inquired
After the shepherd that complained of love,
Who you saw sitting by me on the turf,
Praising the proud disdainful shepherdess
That was his mistress.

Celia   Well, and what of him?

Corin
If you will see a pageant truly played
Between the pale complexion of true love
And the red glow of scorn and proud disdain,
Go hence a little, and I shall conduct you,
If you will mark it.

Rosalind   O, come, let us remove!
The sight of lovers feedeth those in love.
Bring us to this sight, and you shall say
I'll prove a busy actor in their play.   [*Exeunt.*]

3.5 ENTER SILVIUS AND PHOEBE.

Silvius
Sweet Phoebe, do not scorn me, do not, Phoebe!
Say that you love me not, but say not so
In bitterness. The common executioner,
Whose heart th' accustomed sight of death makes hard,
Falls not the ax upon the humbled neck
But first begs pardon. Will you sterner be
Than he that dies and lives by bloody drops?

Enter Rosalind, Celia, and Corin [behind].

Phoebe
    I would not be thy executioner;
    I fly thee, for I would not injure thee.
    Thou tell'st me there is murder in mine eye.
    'Tis pretty, sure, and very probable,
    That eyes, that are the frail'st and softest things,
    Who shut their coward gates on atomies,
    Should be called tyrants, butchers, murderers!
    Now I do frown on thee with all my heart,
    And if mine eyes can wound, now let them kill thee.
    Now counterfeit to swoon; why, now fall down,
    Or if thou canst not, O, for shame, for shame,
    Lie not, to say mine eyes are murderers!
    Now show the wound mine eye hath made in thee.
    Scratch thee but with a pin, and there remains
    Some scar of it; lean upon a rush,
    The cicatrice and capable impressure
    Thy palm some moment keeps; but now mine eyes,
    Which I have darted at thee, hurt thee not,
    Nor, I am sure, there is no force in eyes
    That can do hurt.

Silvius   O dear Phoebe,
    If ever—as that ever may be near—
    You meet in some fresh cheek the power of fancy,
    Then shall you know the wounds invisible
    That love's keen arrows make.

Phoebe   But till that time
    Come not thou near me; and when that time comes,
    Afflict me with thy mocks, pity me not,
    As till that time I shall not pity thee.

Rosalind *[advancing]*
    And why, I pray you? Who might be your mother,
    That you insult, exult, and all at once,
    Over the wretched? What though you have no beauty—
    As, by my faith, I see no more in you

Than without candle may go dark to bed—
Must you be therefore proud and pitiless?
Why, what means this? Why do you look on me?
I see no more in you than in the ordinary
Of nature's sale-work. 'Od's my little life,
I think she means to tangle my eyes too!
No, faith, proud mistress, hope not after it.
'Tis not your inky brows, your black silk hair,
Your bugle eyeballs, nor your cheek of cream
That can entame my spirits to your worship.
[*To Silvius.*]   You foolish shepherd, wherefore do you follow her,
Like foggy south, puffing with wind and rain?
You are a thousand times a properer man
Than she a woman. 'Tis such fools as you
That makes the world full of ill-favored children.
'Tis not her glass, but you, that flatters her,
And out of you she sees herself more proper
Than any of her lineaments can show her.—
But, mistress, know yourself. Down on your knees,
And thank heaven, fasting, for a good man's love!
For I must tell you friendly in your ear,
Sell when you can. You are not for all markets.
Cry the man mercy, love him, take his offer;
Foul is most foul, being foul to be a scoffer.—
So take her to thee, shepherd. Fare you well.

Phoebe

Sweet youth, I pray you, chide a year together.
I had rather hear you chide than this man woo.

Rosalind [*to Phoebe*]   He's fallen in love with your foulness, [*to Silvius*] and she'll fall in love with my anger. If it be so, as fast as she answers thee with frowning looks, I'll sauce her with bitter words. [*To Phoebe.*] Why look you so upon me?

Phoebe   For no ill will I bear you.

Rosalind

I pray you, do not fall in love with me,
For I am falser than vows made in wine.

Besides, I like you not. [*To Silvius.*] If you will know my house,
'Tis at the tuft of olives here hard by.—
Will you go, sister?—Shepherd, ply her hard.—
Come, sister.—Shepherdess, look on him better,
And be not proud. Though all the world could see,
None could be so abused in sight as he.—
Come, to our flock.   *Exit [with Celia and Corin].*

Phoebe

Dead shepherd, now I find thy saw of might,
"Who ever loved that loved not at first sight?"

Silvius

Sweet Phoebe—

Phoebe   Ha, what sayst thou, Silvius?

Silvius   Sweet Phoebe, pity me.

Phoebe

Why, I am sorry for thee, gentle Silvius.

Silvius

Wherever sorrow is, relief would be.
If you do sorrow at my grief in love,
By giving love, your sorrow and my grief
Were both extermined.

Phoebe

Thou hast my love. Is not that neighborly?

Silvius

I would have you.

Phoebe   Why, that were covetousness.
Silvius, the time was that I hated thee,
And yet it is not that I bear thee love;
But since that thou canst talk of love so well,
Thy company, which erst was irksome to me,
I will endure, and I'll employ thee too.
But do not look for further recompense
Than thine own gladness that thou art employed.

Silvius

So holy and so perfect is my love,

And I in such a poverty of grace,
That I shall think it a most plenteous crop
To glean the broken ears after the man
That the main harvest reaps. Loose now and then
A scattered smile, and that I'll live upon.

Phoebe

Know'st thou the youth that spoke to me erewhile?

Silvius

Not very well, but I have met him oft,
And he hath bought the cottage and the bounds
That the old carlot once was master of.

Phoebe

Think not I love him, though I ask for him.
'Tis but a peevish boy—yet he talks well—
But what care I for words? Yet words do well
When he that speaks them pleases those that hear.
It is a pretty youth—not very pretty—
But sure he's proud—and yet his pride becomes him.
He'll make a proper man. The best thing in him
Is his complexion; and faster than his tongue
Did make offense, his eye did heal it up.
He is not very tall—yet for his years he's tall.
His leg is but so-so—and yet 'tis well.
There was a pretty redness in his lip,
A little riper and more lusty red
Than that mixed in his cheek; 'twas just the difference
Betwixt the constant red and mingled damask.
There be some women, Silvius, had they marked him
In parcels as I did, would have gone near
To fall in love with him; but for my part,
I love him not nor hate him not; and yet
I have more cause to hate him than to love him.
For what had he to do to chide at me?
He said mine eyes were black and my hair black
And, now I am remembered, scorned at me.

I marvel why I answered not again.
But that's all one; omittance is no quittance.
I'll write to him a very taunting letter,
And thou shalt bear it. Wilt thou, Silvius?

Silvius

Phoebe, with all my heart.

Phoebe   I'll write it straight;
The matter's in my head and in my heart.
I will be bitter with him and passing short.
Go with me, Silvius.   [*Exeunt.*]

4.1 ENTER ROSALIND AND CELIA, AND JAQUES.

Jaques   I prithee, pretty youth, let me be better acquainted with thee.

Rosalind   They say you are a melancholy fellow.

Jaques   I am so. I do love it better than laughing.

Rosalind   Those that are in extremity of either are abominable fellows and betray themselves to every modern censure worse than drunkards.

Jaques   Why, 'tis good to be sad and say nothing.

Rosalind   Why then, 'tis good to be a post.

Jaques   I have neither the scholar's melancholy, which is emulation, nor the musician's, which is fantastical, nor the courtier's, which is proud, nor the soldier's, which is ambitious, nor the lawyer's, which is politic, nor the lady's, which is nice, nor the lover's, which is all these; but it is a melancholy of mine own, compounded of many simples, extracted from many objects, and indeed the sundry contemplation of my travels, in which my often rumination wraps me in a most humorous sadness.

Rosalind   A traveler! By my faith, you have great reason to be sad. I fear you have sold your own lands to see other men's. Then to have seen much and to have nothing is to have rich eyes and poor hands.

Jaques   Yes, I have gained my experience.

Enter Orlando.

Rosalind And your experience makes you sad. I had rather have a fool to make me merry than experience to make me sad—and to travel for it too!

Orlando Good day and happiness, dear Rosalind!

Jaques Nay, then, God b' wi' you, an you talk in blank verse.

Rosalind Farewell, Monsteur Traveler. Look you lisp and wear strange suits, disable all the benefits of your own country, be out of love with your nativity, and almost chide God for making you that countenance you are, or I will scarce think you have swam in a gondola. [*Exit Jaques.*] Why, how now, Orlando, where have you been all this while? You a lover? An you serve me such another trick, never come in my sight more.

Orlando My fair Rosalind, I come within an hour of my promise.

Rosalind Break an hour's promise in love? He that will divide a minute into a thousand parts and break but a part of the thousandth part of a minute in the affairs of love, it may be said of him that Cupid hath clapped him o' the shoulder, but I'll warrant him heart-whole.

Orlando Pardon me, dear Rosalind.

Rosalind Nay, an you be so tardy, come no more in my sight. I had as lief be wooed of a snail.

Orlando Of a snail?

Rosalind Ay, of a snail; for though he comes slowly, he carries his house on his head—a better jointure, I think, than you make a woman. Besides, he brings his destiny with him.

Orlando What's that?

Rosalind Why, horns, which such as you are fain to be beholding to your wives for. But he comes armed in his fortune and prevents the slander of his wife.

Orlando Virtue is no horn-maker, and my Rosalind is virtuous.

Rosalind And I am your Rosalind.

Celia It pleases him to call you so; but he hath a Rosalind of a better leer than you.

Rosalind   Come, woo me, woo me, for now I am in a holiday humor and like enough to consent. What would you say to me now, an I were your very, very Rosalind?

Orlando   I would kiss before I spoke.

Rosalind   Nay, you were better speak first, and when you were graveled for lack of matter, you might take occasion to kiss. Very good orators, when they are out, they will spit; and for lovers lacking—God warrant us!—matter, the cleanliest shift is to kiss.

Orlando   How if the kiss be denied?

Rosalind   Then she puts you to entreaty, and there begins new matter.

Orlando   Who could be out, being before his beloved mistress?

Rosalind   Marry, that should you, if I were your mistress, or I should think my honesty ranker than my wit.

Orlando   What, of my suit?

Rosalind   Not out of your apparel, and yet out of your suit. Am not I your Rosalind?

Orlando   I take some joy to say you are, because I would be talking of her.

Rosalind   Well, in her person I say I will not have you.

Orlando   Then in mine own person, I die.

Rosalind   No, faith, die by attorney. The poor world is almost six thousand years old, and in all this time there was not any man died in his own person, videlicet, in a love cause. Troilus had his brains dashed out with a Grecian club, yet he did what he could to die before, and he is one of the patterns of love. Leander, he would have lived many a fair year though Hero had turned nun, if it had not been for a hot midsummer night; for, good youth, he went but forth to wash him in the Hellespont and being taken with the cramp was drowned; and me foolish chroniclers of that age found it was—Hero of Sestos. But these are all lies. Men have died from time to time, and worms have eaten them, but not for love.

Orlando   I would not have my right Rosalind of this mind, for I protest her frown might kill me.

Rosalind   By this hand, it will not kill a fly. But come, now I will be your Rosalind in a more coming-on disposition; and ask me what you will, I will grant it.

Orlando	Then love me, Rosalind.
Rosalind	Yes, faith, will I, Fridays and Saturdays and all.
Orlando	And wilt thou have me?
Rosalind	Ay, and twenty such.
Orlando	What sayest thou?
Rosalind	Are you not good?
Orlando	I hope so.

Rosalind   Why then, can one desire too much of a good thing?—Come, sister, you shall be the priest and marry us.—Give me your hand, Orlando.—What do you say, sister?

Orlando   Pray thee, marry us.

Celia   I cannot say the words.

Rosalind   You must begin, "Will you, Orlando—"

Celia   Go to. Will you, Orlando, have to wife this Rosalind?

Orlando   I will.

Rosalind   Ay, but when?

Orlando   Why now, as fast as she can marry us.

Rosalind   Then you must say, "I take thee, Rosalind, for wife."

Orlando   I take thee, Rosalind, for wife.

Rosalind   I might ask you for your commission; but I do take thee, Orlando, for my husband. There's a girl goes before the priest, and certainly a woman's thought runs before her actions.

Orlando   So do all thoughts; they are winged.

Rosalind   Now tell me how long you would have her after you have possessed her.

Orlando   For ever and a day.

Rosalind   Say "a day," without the "ever." No, no, Orlando, men are April when they woo, December when they wed. Maids are May when they are maids, but the sky changes when they are wives. I will be more jealous of thee than a Barbary cock-pigeon over his hen, more clamorous than a parrot against rain, more newfangled than an ape, more giddy in my desires than a monkey. I will weep for nothing, like Diana in the fountain, and I will do that when you are disposed to be merry; I will laugh like a hyena, and that when thou art inclined to sleep.

Orlando   But will my Rosalind do so?

Rosalind   By my life, she will do as I do.

Orlando   O, but she is wise.

Rosalind   Or else she could not have the wit to do this. The wiser, the waywarder. Make the doors upon a woman's wit, and it will out at the casement; shut that, and 'twill out at the keyhole; stop that, 'twill fly with the smoke out at the chimney.

Orlando   A man that had a wife with such a wit, he might say, "Wit, whither wilt?"

Rosalind   Nay, you might keep that check for it till you met your wife's wit going to your neighbor's bed.

Orlando   And what wit could wit have to excuse that?

Rosalind   Marry, to say she came to seek you there. You shall never take her without her answer unless you take her without her tongue. O, that woman that cannot make her fault her husband's occasion, let her never nurse her child herself, for she will breed it like a fool!

Orlando   For these two hours, Rosalind, I will leave thee.

Rosalind   Alas, dear love, I cannot lack thee two hours!

Orlando   I must attend the Duke at dinner. By two o'clock I will be with thee again.

Rosalind   Ay, go your ways, go your ways. I knew what you would prove. My friends told me as much, and I thought no less. That flattering tongue of yours won me. 'Tis but one cast away, and so, come, death! Two o'clock is your hour?

Orlando   Ay, sweet Rosalind.

Rosalind   By my troth, and in good earnest, and so God mend me, and by all pretty oaths that are not dangerous, if you break one jot of your promise or come one minute behind your hour, I will think you the most pathetical break-promise, and the most hollow lover, and the most unworthy of her you call Rosalind, that may be chosen out of the gross band of the unfaithful. Therefore beware my censure, and keep your promise.

Orlando   With no less religion than if thou wert indeed my Rosalind. So adieu.

Rosalind   Well, Time is the old justice that examines all such of-
fenders, and let Time try. Adieu.

Exit [Orlando].

Celia   You have simply misused our sex in your love prate. We must
have your doublet and hose plucked over your head and show the
world what the bird hath done to her own nest.

Rosalind   O coz, coz, coz, my pretty little coz, that thou didst know
how many fathom deep I am in love! But it cannot be sounded; my
affection hath an unknown bottom, like the Bay of Portugal.

Celia   Or rather, bottomless, that as fast as you pour affection in, it
runs out.

Rosalind   No, that same wicked bastard of Venus, that was begot of
thought, conceived of spleen, and born of madness, that blind ras-
cally boy that abuses every-one's eyes because his own are out, let
him be judge how deep I am in love. I'll tell thee, Aliena, I cannot
be out of the sight of Orlando. I'll go find a shadow and sigh till he
come.

Celia   And I'll sleep.   [*Exeunt.*]

4.2 ENTER JAQUES AND LORDS [DRESSED AS] FORESTERS.

Jaques   Which is he that killed the deer?

First Lord   Sir, it was I.

Jaques   Let's present him to the Duke, like a Roman conqueror, and
it would do well to set the deer's horns upon his head for a branch
of victory. Have you no song, Forester, for this purpose?

Second Lord   Yes, sir.

Jaques   Sing it. 'Tis no matter how it be in tune, so it a make noise
enough.   [*Music.*]

Song.

Second Lord [*sings*]

What shall he have that killed the deer?
His leather skin and horns to wear.
Then sing him home; the rest shall bear

This burden.
Take thou no scorn to wear the horn;
It was a crest ere thou wast born.
Thy father's father wore it,
And thy father bore it.
The horn, the horn, the lusty horn
Is not a thing to laugh to scorn.

[Exeunt.]

4.3 ENTER ROSALIND AND CELIA.

Rosalind   How say you now? Is it not past two o'clock? And here much
Orlando!

Celia   I warrant you, with pure love and troubled brain he hath ta'en
his bow and arrows and is gone forth—to sleep.

Enter Silvius [with a letter].

Look who comes here.

Silvius [to Rosalind]
My errand is to you, fair youth.
My gentle Phoebe bid me give you this.

[He gives the letter.]

I know not the contents, but as I guess
By the stern brow and waspish action
Which she did use as she was writing of it,
It bears an angry tenor. Pardon me;
I am but as a guiltless messenger.

Rosalind [examining the letter]
Patience herself would startle at this letter
And play the swaggerer. Bear this, bear all!
She says I am not fair, that I lack manners;
She calls me proud, and that she could not love me
Were man as rare as phoenix. 'Od's my will!
Her love is not the hare that I do hunt.
Why writes she so to me? Well, shepherd, well,
This is a letter of your own device.

Silvius
　　No, I protest, I know not the contents.
　　Phoebe did write it.
Rosalind　　　　　　　Come, come, you are a fool,
　　And turned into the extremity of love.
　　I saw her hand; she has a leathern hand,
　　A freestone-colored hand. I verily did think
　　That her old gloves were on, but 'twas her hands;
　　She has a huswife's hand—but that's no matter.
　　I say she never did invent this letter;
　　This is a man's invention and his hand.
Silvius　　Sure it is hers.

Rosalind

> Why, 'tis a boisterous and a cruel style,
> A style for challengers. Why, she defies me,
> Like Turk to Christian. Women's gentle brain
> Could not drop forth such giant-rude invention,
> Such Ethiop words, blacker in their effect
> Than in their countenance. Will you hear the letter?

Silvius

> So please you, for I never heard it yet;
> Yet, heard too much of Phoebe's cruelty.

Rosalind

> She Phoebes me. Mark how the tyrant writes.   [*Read.*]
>> "Art thou god to shepherd turned,
>> That a maiden's heart hath burned?"
> Can a woman rail thus?

Silvius   Call you this railing?

Rosalind   [*Read.*]
>> "Why, thy godhead laid apart,
>> Warr'st thou with a woman's heart?"
> Did you ever hear such railing?
>> "Whiles the eye of man did woo me,
>> That could do no vengeance to me."—
> Meaning me a beast.
>> "If the scorn of your bright eyne
>> Have power to raise such love in mine,
>> Alack, in me what strange effect
>> Would they work in mild aspect!
>> Whiles you chid me, I did love;
>> How then might your prayers move!
>> He that brings this love to thee
>> Little knows this love in me;
>> And by him seal up thy mind,
>> Whether that thy youth and kind
>> Will the faithful offer take
>> Of me and all that I can make,

 Or else by him my love deny,
 And then I'll study how to die."

Silvius   Call you this chiding?

Celia   Alas, poor shepherd!

Rosalind   Do you pity him? No, he deserves no pity.—Wilt thou love such a woman? What, to make thee an instrument and play false strains upon thee? Not to be endured! Well, go your way to her, for I see love hath made thee a tame snake, and say this to her: that if she love me, I charge her to love thee; if she will not, I will never have her unless thou entreat for her. If you be a true lover, hence, and not a word; for here comes more company.   [*Exit Silvius.*]

Enter Oliver.

Oliver

 Good morrow, fair ones. Pray you, if you know,
 Where in the purlieus of this forest stands
 A sheepcote fenced about with olive trees?

Celia

 West of this place, down in the neighbor bottom;
 The rank of osiers by the murmuring stream
 Left on your right hand brings you to the place.
 But at this hour the house doth keep itself;
 There's none within.

Oliver

 If that an eye may profit by a tongue,
 Then should I know you by description,
 Such garments and such years: "The boy is fair,
 Of female favor, and bestows himself
 Like a ripe sister; the woman, low
 And browner than her brother." Are not you
 The owner of the house I did inquire for?

Celia

 It is no boast, being asked, to say we are.

Oliver

 Orlando doth commend him to you both,

And to that youth he calls his Rosalind
He sends this bloody napkin. Are you he?

> [*He produces a bloody handkerchief.*]

Rosalind

I am. What must we understand by this?

Oliver

Some of my shame, if you will know of me
What man I am, and how, and why, and where
This handkerchief was stained.

Celia   I pray you, tell it.

Oliver

When last the young Orlando parted from you
He left a promise to return again
Within an hour, and, pacing through the forest,
Chewing the food of sweet and bitter fancy,
Lo, what befell! He threw his eye aside,
And mark what object did present itself:
Under an old oak, whose boughs were mossed with age
And high top bald with dry antiquity,
A wretched, ragged man, o'ergrown with hair,
Lay sleeping on his back. About his neck
A green and gilded snake had wreathed itself,
Who with her head, nimble in threats, approached
The opening of his mouth; but suddenly,
Seeing Orlando, it unlinked itself
And with indented glides did slip away
Into a bush, under which bush's shade
A lioness, with udders all drawn dry,
Lay couching, head on ground, with catlike watch,
When that the sleeping man should stir; for 'tis
The royal disposition of that beast
To prey on nothing that doth seem as dead.
This seen, Orlando did approach the man
And found it was his brother, his elder brother.

Celia

O, I have heard him speak of that same brother,

And he did render him the most unnatural
That lived amongst men.

Oliver   And well he might so do,
For well I know he was unnatural.

Rosalind
But to Orlando: did he leave him there,
Food to the sucked and hungry lioness?

Oliver
Twice did he turn his back and purposed so;
But kindness, nobler ever than revenge,
And nature, stronger than his just occasion,
Made him give battle to the lioness,
Who quickly fell before him; in which hurtling
From miserable slumber I awaked.

Celia
Are you his brother?

Rosalind   Was 't you he rescued?

Celia
Was 't you that did so oft contrive to kill him?

Oliver
'Twas I, but 'tis not I. I do not shame
To tell you what I was, since my conversion
So sweetly tastes, being the thing I am.

Rosalind
But for the bloody napkin?

Oliver   By and by.
When from the first to last betwixt us two
Tears our recountments had most kindly bathed,
As how I came into that desert place,
In brief, he led me to the gentle Duke,
Who gave me fresh array and entertainment,
Committing me unto my brother's love;
Who led me instantly unto his cave,
There stripped himself, and here upon his arm
The lioness had torn some flesh away,
Which all this while had bled; and now he fainted

And cried, in fainting, upon Rosalind.
Brief, I recovered him, bound up his wound,
And after some small space, being strong at heart,
He sent me hither, stranger as I am,
To tell this story, that you might excuse
His broken promise, and to give this napkin
Dyed in his blood unto the shepherd youth
That he in sport doth call his Rosalind.

[*Rosalind swoons.*]

Celia

Why, how now, Ganymede, sweet Ganymede!

Oliver

Many will swoon when they do look on blood.

Celia

There is more in it.—Cousin Ganymede!

Oliver   Look, he recovers.

Rosalind   I would I were at home.

Celia   We'll lead you thither.—
I pray you, will you take him by the arm?

[*They help Rosalind up.*]

Oliver   Be of good cheer, youth. You a man? You lack a man's heart.

Rosalind   I do so, I confess it. Ah, sirrah, a body would think this was
well counterfeited. I pray you, tell your brother how well I counterfeited. Heigh-ho!

Oliver   This was not counterfeit. There is too great testimony in your
complexion that it was a passion of earnest.

Rosalind   Counterfeit, I assure you.

Oliver   Well then, take a good heart and counterfeit to be a man.

Rosalind   So I do; but, i' faith, I should have been a woman by right.

Celia   Come, you look paler and paler. Pray you, draw homewards.—
Good sir, go with us.

Oliver

That will I, for I must bear answer back
How you excuse my brother, Rosalind.

Rosalind   I shall devise something. But, I pray you, commend my counterfeiting to him. Will you go?

[*Exeunt.*]

5.1 ENTER [*TOUCHSTONE THE*] CLOWN AND AUDREY.

Touchstone   We shall find a time, Audrey. Patience, gentle Audrey.

Audrey   Faith, the priest was good enough, for all the old gentleman's saying.

Touchstone   A most wicked Sir Oliver, Audrey, a most vile Mar-text. But Audrey, there is a youth here in the forest lays claim to you.

Audrey   Ay, I know who 'tis. He hath no interest in me in the world. Here comes the man you mean.

Enter William.

Touchstone   It is meat and drink to me to see a clown. By my troth, we that have good wits have much to answer for. We shall be flouting; we cannot hold.

William   Good even, Audrey.

Audrey   God gi' good even, William.

William   And good even to you, sir.

[*He removes his hat.*]

Touchstone   Good even, gentle friend. Cover thy head, cover thy head. Nay, prithee be covered. How old are you, friend?

William   Five-and-twenty, sir.

Touchstone   A ripe age. Is thy name William?

William   William, sir.

Touchstone   A fair name. Wast born i' the forest here?

William   Ay, sir, I thank God.

Touchstone   "Thank God"—a good answer. Art rich?

William   Faith, sir, so-so.

Touchstone   "So-so" is good, very good, very excellent good; and yet it is not, it is but so-so. Art thou wise?

William   Ay, sir, I have a pretty wit.

Touchstone   Why, thou sayst well. I do now remember a saying, "The fool doth think he is wise, but the wise man knows himself to be a fool." The heathen philosopher, when he had a desire to eat a grape, would open his lips when he put it into his mouth, meaning thereby that grapes were made to eat and lips to open. You do love this maid?

William   I do, sir.

Touchstone   Give me your hand. Art thou learned?

William   No, sir.

Touchstone   Then learn this of me: to have is to have. For it is a figure in rhetoric that drink, being poured out of a cup into a glass, by filling the one doth empty the other. For all your writers do consent that *ipse* is he. Now, you are not *ipse*, for I am he.

William   Which he, sir?

Touchstone   He, sir, that must marry this woman. Therefore, you clown, abandon—which is in the vulgar "leave"—the society—which in the boorish is "company"—of this female—which in the common is "woman"; which together is, abandon the society of this female, or, clown, thou perishest; or, to thy better understanding, diest; or, to wit, I kill thee, make thee away, translate thy life into death, thy liberty into bondage. I will deal in poison with thee, or in bastinado, or in steel; I will bandy with thee in faction, I will o'errun thee with policy; I will kill thee a hundred and fifty ways. Therefore tremble, and depart.

Audrey   Do, good William.

William   God rest you merry, sir.   [*Exit.*]

Enter Corin.

Corin   Our master and mistress seeks you. Come, away, away!

Touchstone   Trip, Audrey, trip, Audrey!—I attend, I attend.   [*Exeunt.*]

5.2 ENTER ORLANDO [*WITH HIS WOUNDED ARM IN A SLING*]
AND OLIVER.

Orlando   Is 't possible that on so little acquaintance you should like her? That but seeing, you should love her? And loving, woo? And, wooing, she should grant? And will you persevere to enjoy her?

Oliver   Neither call the giddiness of it in question, the poverty of her, the small acquaintance, my sudden wooing, nor her sudden consenting; but say with me, "I love Aliena"; say with her that she loves me; consent with both that we may enjoy each other. It shall be to your good; for my father's house and all the revenue that was old Sir Rowland's will I estate upon you, and here live and die a shepherd.

Enter Rosalind.

Orlando   You have my consent. Let your wedding be tomorrow. Thither will I invite the Duke and all 's contented followers. Go you and prepare Aliena; for look you, here comes my Rosalind.

Rosalind   God save you, brother.

Oliver   And you, fair sister.   [*Exit.*]

Rosalind   O my dear Orlando, how it grieves me to see thee wear thy heart in a scarf!

Orlando   It is my arm.

Rosalind   I thought thy heart had been wounded with the claws of a lion.

Orlando   Wounded it is, but with the eyes of a lady.

Rosalind   Did your brother tell you how I counterfeited to swoon when he showed me your handkerchief?

Orlando   Ay, and greater wonders than that.

Rosalind   O I know where you are. Nay, 'tis true. There was never anything so sudden but the fight of two rams and Caesar's thrasonical brag of "I came, saw, and overcame." For your brother and my sister no sooner met but they looked, no sooner looked but they loved, no sooner loved but they sighed, no sooner sighed but they asked one another the reason, no sooner knew the reason but they sought the remedy; and in these degrees have they made a pair of stairs to marriage which they will climb incontinent, or else be incontinent before marriage. They are in the very wrath of love, and they will together. Clubs cannot part them.

Orlando   They shall be married tomorrow, and I will bid the Duke to the nuptial. But O, how bitter a thing it is to look into happiness through another man's eyes! By so much the more shall I tomorrow be at the height of heart-heaviness, by how much I shall think my brother happy in having what he wishes for.

Rosalind   Why, then, tomorrow I cannot serve your turn for Rosalind?

Orlando   I can live no longer by thinking.

Rosalind   I will weary you then no longer with idle talking. Know of me then—for now I speak to some purpose—that I know you are a gentleman of good conceit. I speak not this that you should bear a good opinion of my knowledge, insomuch I say I know you are; neither do I labor for a greater esteem than may in some little measure draw a belief from you to do yourself good and not to grace me. Believe then, if you please, that I can do strange things. I have, since I was three years old, conversed with a magician, most profound in his art and yet not damnable. If you do love Rosalind so near the heart as your gesture cries it out, when your brother marries Aliena shall you marry her. I know into what straits of fortune she is driven; and it is not impossible to me, if it appear not inconvenient to you, to set her before your eyes tomorrow, human as she is, and without any danger.

Orlando   Speak'st thou in sober meanings?

Rosalind   By my life, I do, which I tender dearly, though I say I am a magician. Therefore, put you in your best array; bid your friends; for if you will be married tomorrow, you shall, and to Rosalind, if you will.

Enter Silvius and Phoebe.

Look, here comes a lover of mine and a lover of hers.

Phoebe [to Rosalind]
    Youth, you have done me much ungentleness,
    To show the letter that I writ to you.

Rosalind
    I care not if I have. It is my study
    To seem despiteful and ungentle to you.
    You are there followed by a faithful shepherd.
    Look upon him; love him. He worships you.

Phoebe [to Silvius]
    Good shepherd, tell this youth what 'tis to love.

Silvius
    It is to be all made of sighs and tears;

And so am I for Phoebe.

Phoebe   And I for Ganymede.

Orlando   And I for Rosalind.

Rosalind   And I for no woman.

Silvius

It is to be all made of faith and service;

And so am I for Phoebe.

Phoebe   And I for Ganymede.

Orlando   And I for Rosalind.

Rosalind   And I for no woman.

Silvius

It is to be all made of fantasy,

All made of passion and all made of wishes,

All adoration, duty, and observance,

All humbleness, all patience and impatience,

All purity, all trial, all observance;

And so am I for Phoebe.

Phoebe   And so am I for Ganymede.

Orlando   And so am I for Rosalind.

Rosalind   And so am I for no woman.

Phoebe [*to Rosalind*]

If this be so, why blame you me to love you?

Silvius [*to Phoebe*]

If this be so, why blame you me to love you?

Orlando

If this be so, why blame you me to love you?

Rosalind   Why do you speak too, "Why blame you me to love you?"

Orlando   To her that is not here, nor doth not hear.

Rosalind   Pray you, no more of this; 'tis like the howling of Irish wolves against the moon. [*To Silvius.*] I will help you, if I can. [*To Phoebe.*] I would love you, if I could.—Tomorrow meet me all together. [*To Phoebe.*] I will marry you, if ever I marry woman, and I'll be married tomorrow. [*To Orlando.*] I will satisfy you, if ever I satisfied man, and you shall be married tomorrow. [*To Silvius.*] I will content you, if what pleases you contents you, and you shall be married tomorrow. [*To Orlando.*] As you love Rosalind, meet.

[*To Silvius.*] As you love Phoebe, meet. And as I love no woman, I'll meet. So fare you well. I have left you commands.

Silvius   I'll not fail, if I live.

Phoebe   Nor I.

Orlando   Nor I.   *Exeunt [separately].*

5.3 ENTER [TOUCHSTONE THE] CLOWN AND AUDREY.

Touchstone   Tomorrow is the joyful day, Audrey; tomorrow will we be married.

Audrey   I do desire it with all my heart; and I hope it is no dishonest desire to desire to be a woman of the world. Here come two of the banished Duke's pages.

Enter two Pages.

First Page   Well met, honest gentleman.

Touchstone   By my troth, well met. Come, sit, sit, and a song.

                                                                [They sit]

Second Page   We are for you. Sit i' the middle.

First Page   Shall we clap into 't roundly, without hawking or spitting or saying we are hoarse, which are the only prologues to a bad voice?

Second Page   I' faith, i' faith, and both in a tune, like two gypsies on a horse.

Song.

Both Pages

    It was a lover and his lass,
        With a hey, and a ho, and a hey-nonny-no,
    That o'er the green cornfield did pass
        In springtime, the only pretty ring time,
    When birds do sing, hey ding a ding, ding,
    Sweet lovers love the spring.

    Between the acres of the rye,
        With a hey, and a ho, and a hey-nonny-no,

These pretty country folks would lie
 In springtime, the only pretty ring time,
When birds do sing, hey ding a ding, ding,
Sweet lovers love the spring.

This carol they began that hour,
 With a hey, and a ho, and hey-nonny-no,
How that a life was but a flower
 In springtime, the only pretty ring time,
When birds do sing, hey ding a ding, ding,
Sweet lovers love the spring.

And therefore take the present time,
 With a hey, and a ho, and a hey-nonny-no;
For love is crowned with the prime
 In springtime, the only pretty ring time,
When birds do sing, hey ding a ding, ding,
Sweet lovers love the spring.

Touchstone Truly, young gentlemen, though there was no great matter in the ditty, yet the note was very untunable.
First Page You are deceived, sir. We kept time, we lost not our time.
Touchstone By my troth, yes; I count it but time lost to hear such a foolish song. God b' wi' you, and God mend your voices! Come, Audrey. *Exeunt [separately].*

5.4 Enter Duke Senior, Amiens, Jaques, Orlando,
Oliver, [and] Celia.

Duke Senior
 Dost thou believe, Orlando, that the boy
 Can do all this that he hath promisèd?
Orlando
 I sometimes do believe, and sometimes do not,
 As those that fear they hope and know they fear.

Enter Rosalind, Silvius, and Phoebe.

Rosalind

Patience once more, whiles our compact is urged.
[*To the Duke.*]   You say, if I bring in your Rosalind
You will bestow her on Orlando here?

Duke Senior

That would I, had I kingdoms to give with her.

Rosalind [*to Orlando*]

And you say you will have her when I bring her?

Orlando

That would I, were I of all kingdoms king.

Rosalind [*to Phoebe*]

You say you'll marry me if I be willing?

Phoebe

That will I, should I die the hour after.

Rosalind

But if you do refuse to marry me
You'll give yourself to this most faithful shepherd?

Phoebe   So is the bargain.

Rosalind [*to Silvius*]

You say that you'll have Phoebe if she will?

Silvius

Though to have her and death were both one thing.

Rosalind

I have promised to make all this matter even.
Keep you your word, O Duke, to give your daughter;
You yours, Orlando, to receive his daughter;
Keep you your word, Phoebe, that you'll marry me,
Or else, refusing me, to wed this shepherd;
Keep your word, Silvius, that you'll marry her
If she refuse me; and from hence I go,
To make these doubts all even.

[*Exeunt Rosalind and Celia.*]

Duke Senior

I do remember in this shepherd boy

Some lively touches of my daughter's favor.
Orlando
    My lord, the first tune that I ever saw him
    Methought he was a brother to your daughter.
    But, my good lord, this boy is forest-born
    And hath been tutored in the rudiments
    Of many desperate studies by his uncle,
    Whom he reports to be a great magician,
    Obscurèd in the circle of this forest.

Enter [Touchstone the] Clown and Audrey.

Jaques There is, sure, another flood toward, and these couples are coming to the ark. Here comes a pair of very strange beasts, which in all tongues are called fools.

Touchstone Salutation and greeting to you all!

Jaques Good my lord, bid him welcome. This is the motley-minded gentleman that I have so often met in the forest. He hath been a courtier, he swears.

Touchstone If any man doubt that, let him put me to my purgation. I have trod a measure; I have flattered a lady; I have been politic with my friend, smooth with mine enemy; I have undone three tailors; I have had four quarrels and like to have fought one.

Jaques And how was that ta'en up?

Touchstone Faith, we met and found the quarrel was upon the seventh cause.

Jaques How seventh cause?—Good my lord, like this fellow.

Duke Senior I like him very well.

Touchstone God 'ild you, sir, I desire you of the like. I press in here, sir, amongst the rest of the country copulatives, to swear and to forswear, according as marriage binds and blood breaks. A poor virgin, sir, an ill-favored thing, sir, but mine own; a poor humor of mine, sir, to take that that no man else will. Rich honesty dwells like a miser, sir, in a poor house, as your pearl in your foul oyster.

Duke Senior By my faith, he is why swift and sententious.

Touchstone According to the fool's bolt, sir, and such dulcet diseases.

Jaques But for the seventh cause. How did you find the quarrel on the seventh cause?

Touchstone Upon a lie seven times removed—bear your body more seeming, Audrey—as thus, sir. I did dislike the cut of a certain courtier's beard. He sent me word if I said his beard was not cut well, he was in the mind it was: this is called the Retort Courteous. If I sent him word again it was not well cut, he would send me word he cut it to please himself: this is called the Quip Modest. If again it was not well cut, he disabled my judgment: this is called the Reply Churlish. If again it was not well cut, he would answer I spake not true: this is called the Reproof Valiant. If again it was not well cut, he would say I lie: this is called the Countercheck Quarrelsome. And so to the Lie Circumstantial and the Lie Direct.

Jaques   And how oft did you say his beard was not well cut?

Touchstone   I durst go no further than the Lie Circumstantial, nor he durst not give me the Lie Direct; and so we measured swords and parted.

Jaques   Can you nominate in order now the degrees of the lie?

Touchstone   O sir, we quarrel in print, by the book, as you have books for good manners. I will name you the degrees. The first, the Retort Courteous; the second, the Quip Modest; the third, the Reply Churlish; the fourth, the Reproof Valiant; the fifth, the Countercheck Quarrelsome; the sixth, the Lie with Circumstance; the seventh, the Lie Direct. All these you may avoid but the Lie Direct; and you may avoid that, too, with an If. I knew when seven justices could not take up a quarrel, but when the parties were met themselves, one of them thought but of an If, as, "If you said so, then I said so"; and they shook hands and swore brothers. Your If is the only peacemaker; much virtue in If.

Jaques   Is not this a rare fellow, my lord? He's as good at anything and yet a fool.

Duke Senior   He uses his folly like a stalking-horse, and under the presentation of that he shoots his wit.

Enter Hymen, Rosalind, and Celia. Still music.
[Rosalind and Celia are no longer disguised.]

Hymen

> Then is there mirth in heaven,
> When earthly things made even
>   Atone together.
> Good Duke, receive thy daughter;
> Hymen from heaven brought her,
>   Yea, brought her hither,
> That thou mightst join her hand with his
> Whose heart within his bosom is.

Rosalind [*to the Duke*]
    To you I give myself, for I am yours.
    [*To Orlando.*] To you I give myself, for I am yours.
Duke Senior
    If there be truth in sight, you are my daughter.
Orlando
    If there be truth in sight, you are my Rosalind.
Phoebe
    If sight and shape be true,
    Why then, my love adieu!
Rosalind [*to the Duke*]
    I'll have no father, if you be not he.
    [*To Orlando.*] I'll have no husband, if you be not he.
    [*To Phoebe.*] Nor ne'er wed woman, if you be not she.
Hymen
        Peace, ho! I bar confusion.
        'Tis I must make conclusion
          Of these most strange events.
        Here's eight that must take hands
        To join in Hymen's bands,
          If truth holds true contents.
    [*To Orlando and Rosalind.*]
        You and you no cross shall part.
    [*To Oliver and Celia.*]
        You and you are heart in heart.
    [*To Phoebe.*]
        You to his love must accord
        Or have a woman to your lord.
    [*To Touchstone and Audrey.*]
        You and you are sure together,
        As the winter to foul weather.
    [*To All.*]
        Whiles a wedlock hymn we sing,
        Feed yourselves with questioning,
        That reason wonder may diminish
        How thus we met, and these things finish.

Song.

Wedding is great Juno's crown,
    O blessèd bond of board and bed!
'Tis Hymen peoples every town;
    High wedlock then be honorèd.
Honor, high honor and renown
    To Hymen, god of every town!

Duke Senior [*to Celia*]
    O my dear niece, welcome thou art to me!
    Even daughter, welcome, in no less degree.
Phoebe [*to Silvius*]
    I will not eat my word, now thou art mine;
    Thy faith my fancy to thee doth combine.

Enter Second Brother [*Jaques de Boys*].

Jaques de Boys
    Let me have audience for a word or two.
    I am the second son of old Sir Rowland,
    That bring these tidings to this fair assembly.
    Duke Frederick, hearing how that every day
    Men of great worth resorted to this forest,
    Addressed a mighty power, which were on foot
    In his own conduct, purposely to take
    His brother here and put him to the sword;
    And to the skirts of this wild wood he came,
    Where, meeting with an old religious man,
    After some question with him, was converted
    Both from his enterprise and from the world,
    His crown bequeathing to his banished brother,
    And all their lands restored to them again
    That were with him exiled. This to be true
    I do engage my life.
Duke Senior   Welcome, young man.
    Thou offer'st fairly to thy brothers' wedding:
    To one his lands withheld and to the other

A land itself at large, a potent dukedom.
First, in this forest let us do those ends
That here were well begun and well begot;
And after, every of this happy number
That have endured shrewd days and nights with us
Shall share the good of our returnèd fortune
According to the measure of their states.
Meantime, forget this new-fall'n dignity,
And fall into our rustic revelry.
Play, music! And you, brides and bridegrooms all,
With measure heaped in joy, to th' measures fall.

Jaques

Sir, by your patience.—If I heard you rightly,
The Duke hath put on a religious life
And thrown into neglect the pompous court.

Jaques de Boys   He hath.

Jaques

To him will I. Out of these convertites
There is much matter to be heard and learned.
[*To the Duke.*] You to your former honor I bequeath;
Your patience and your virtue well deserves it.
[*To Orlando.*] You to a love that your true faith doth merit;
[*To Oliver*] You to your land and love and great allies;
[*To Silvius*] You to a long and well-deservèd bed;
[*To Touchstone*] And you to wrangling, for my loving voyage
Is but for two months victualed. So, to your pleasures.
I am for other than for dancing measures.

Duke Senior   Stay, Jaques, stay.

Jaques

To see no pastime I. What you would have
I'll stay to know at your abandoned cave.   [*Exit.*]

Duke Senior

Proceed, proceed. We'll begin these rites,
As we do trust they'll end, in true delights.

                                    [*They dance.*] *Exeunt* [*all but Rosalind*].

EPILOGUE

Rosalind   It is not the fashion to see the lady the epilogue; but it is no more unhandsome than to see the lord the prologue. If it be true that good wine needs no bush, 'tis true that a good play needs no epilogue. Yet to good wine they do use good bushes, and good plays prove the better by the help of good epilogues. What a case am I in then, that am neither a good epilogue nor cannot insinuate with you in the behalf of a good play! I am not furnished like a beggar; therefore to beg will not become me. My way is to conjure you, and I'll begin with the women. I charge you, O women, for the love you bear to men, to like as much of this play as please you; and I charge you, O men, for the love you bear to women—as I perceive by your simpering, none of you hates them—that between you and the women the play may please. If I were a woman I would kiss as many of you as had beards that pleased me, complexions that liked me, and breaths that I defied not; and I am sure as many as have good beards or good faces or sweet breaths will, for my kind offer, when I make curtsy, bid me farewell.   [*Exit.*]